LEMADY

Episodes of a Writer's Life

by Keith Roberts

WILDSIDE PRESS
Berkeley Heights, NJ ▼ 1999

WILDSIDE PRESS
P.O. Box 45
Gillette, NJ 07933-0045

CONTENTS

DEDICATION

For Jayne, Stuart,
Ben and Kelly

I.

We are driving the Great West Road. The car is sounding good. It should do; it only has a few thousand on the clock. The last Spitfire was a teabreak special; rust holes had developed in the body sills that you could have thrown your hat through. I made some enquiries, took it to a recommended spray shop. Chancing my arm, I asked if they could give it a dealer's skim. The man addressed narrowed his eyes, looked at me sharply.

"On one condition. Don't bring it back."

"I shan't bring it back."

I got list price for the heap. The salesman, so-called, was amiable but purblind. He said it was obvious it had been well maintained. For once I felt no guilt. *Caveat emptor*; and in any case I had no cause to love the establishment he served. It made a change to come out on the winning side. The new car is to rot in turn; but not for a little while.

Lemady is with me. She is wearing light blue slacks, a vivid matching blouse. Her blonde hair blows forward in a heavy cloud. Sunglasses are propped on her nose, and she is reading a paper. A few miles back we stopped at a wayside showroom to gloat over the stock: a line of glinting motors, each a post-vintage thoroughbred. Now we are headed for Dorset.

There are times, and this is one of them, when one is conscious that a key Image has been formed. The elegant woman, the bright road ahead; the stuff of Sunday supplements, perhaps. But real for all that. Naturally, it is to fade; as the Gotama warned, all States are subject to Change. But not beyond recall. For me, Lemady is still in the car.

The name I have chosen for her needs a touch of explanation. For reasons both tedious and predictable, I had no wish to identify her more closely; but there was another purpose. Lemady informed all but a couple of my books; I wanted to hint somehow at that universality. At first, I thought simply of "The Woman." After all, it was good enough for Sherlock Holmes; the opera singer who quite early on made rings round him was later accorded the title. But on reflection it seemed insufferably pompous. Lemady, the subject of one of Britten's spare, bony little folk settings, seemed altogether more human and approachable. Also the letters can be adjusted, amusingly, to form elements of Lemady's own name. Name magic remains a potent force, even in these enlightened times.

Potent indeed. Years later I am to hear the personnel of Kerosina, the limited edition company I basically set running, all but came
to blows over who was to be accorded which of the lettered, leather-
bound copies; each wanted their own initial. So in one respect at least
they displayed energy. I was still beavering away on the production of
their first title; so the effect was rather like vivisecting the infant before
it was born. Something more detailed than the Judgment of Solomon
seemed called for; but that lies in the future.

Folk song, like folk culture in general, is a vast field, and carries its own dangers. Quite early on, as a result of the "Anita" pieces, a
comedy witchcraft series set on my own once-native heath, I was dismissed by one editor as "that folksy guy." People love labels. Classifi-
cation, whether accurate or not, equates with safety; that which is pigeonholed can be more readily dismissed. But all things twine and interweave. Lemady, with her flying hair, her sophistication, has the
Sight; or so she claims. It comes on her at unexpected moments; and it
frightens her. "If you had it," she tells me once, "you would wish you
hadn't." Classify that.

Rob Holdstock, in his introduction to my ghost collection,
partly revives the folksy image. Though I have no complaint. To be
described as a folklorist in every sense is after all a pretty good compliment. Folklore is part of the experience of us all, whether we like it
or not. Again, it's the pigeonhole mentality that insists on trying to set
it apart.

The composer Constant Lambert said once that after you had
played a folk song all you could really do was play it again, louder.
The remark is a little tongue-in-cheek; by all reports he was a pal of
Britten's anyway, it was a wrangle they must often have had. Also, it
contains a kernel of truth. If the essence of peasant art is overlapping
decoration (Barbara Jones: *The Unsophisticated Arts*. Who remembers
that classic book now; come to that, how many of today's readers ever
heard of it?) then the essence of folk song is repetition, allied to the
construction of curiously long melodic units. Vaughan-Williams was
one of the few composers who, it seemed, could produce them at will.
The haunting *Linden Lea* is a classic example; he did it again in the
middle of *The Lark Ascending*.

Lemady is a long melodic unit. She missed six feet by an
inch; in her teens, it disappointed her. Now though she says she
doesn't mind. She tucks her shoulder under my arm sometimes; she
says it makes her feel more in proportion. As in all things, her response is complex. Her independence of spirit gives way at times to a
seeming desire for compliance, a need to play second string; though it
is as dangerous as it would be undesirable to take her attitude for
granted. She is made up of opposites; withdrawn by nature, she can
still play the Scarlet Woman with the best; if she is sufficiently riled, or
feels herself under attack. I had known her for some time when she ap-

peared one morning in a spitting rage. A tax demand had been made against her; she considered it unjust. "There's only two ways to make money in this country," she snapped. "Win it, or—beep—steal it." Before my jaw had properly finished sagging, she had marched into a bookies. She slapped two pounds on the nose of an outsider; to this day, I don't know how to fill in a betting slip. "We'll pick the winnings up later," she said decisively. "Then you can take me out." The horse romped home. She seemed unsurprised. I have no idea what guided her choice; nor did she ever do such a thing again. In my company at least.

My dislike of bookmakers' establishments doesn't spring from a finely-tuned moral sense. The carefully blanked-out windows, the endless roaring of the racing commentaries, clearly audible from the street, hold no appeal. While I was never bitten by the gambling bug, I have heard the compulsion springs from dissatisfaction with one's lot, the urgent need somehow to change one's fortunes; and that may be so of course. Hence, presumably, the fascination of fruit machines, with their promise of lightning-fast fluctuations of chance.

Sprinkler Sam offers a classic example of the addiction. He's elderly, on the deaf side and employed as a KP at the local Country Club. On pay nights he heads for town with his pathetic handful of notes. So keenly has the compulsion gripped him that once on a machine he won't risk leaving it, even to go to the loo; he'd sooner piddle himself. As a result he's banned from most of the pubs and bars in town. Except one. There, the landlord keeps a special strip of carpet; it's laid in preparation for the performance, then solemnly taken out and dried ready for next week. Hearing the nickname, a new barmaid is intrigued. She asks me how it was acquired.

"You just watch the floor round his feet. You'll soon find out."

The ensuing performance is one of Sam's more spectacular efforts. Her eyes widen progressively with shock. Halfway through, a lady appears. She represents the excellent Lifeboat Fund; she would like to leave one of the well-known collection boxes on the bar. The landlord declines. For him, all charities begin at home.

"I think you'd better have one, Edward. If he goes on like that, we're all going to *need* a bloody lifeboat...."

The barmaid makes a strangled sort of sound, and exits.

On occasions, the addiction acquires more sinister overtones. While working in Reading I'm assailed by an account executive, so-called, who I cordially detest. The day before, I had annoyed him considerably. We had been ordered to attend a function held at the offices of a newly taken-over newspaper, at which as it transpired the advertising staff of the area were to be told how they were collectively going to be run out of business, news my employer of the time greeted with a thin smile. His grandfather had been a mayor of the town; he was ensconced very firmly on the Square.

My executive acquaintance announced, with an habitual twisting of his curiously weak little mouth, that I would have to make my own way to the event. It would be a bit of a walk; the venue was on the other side of town. It couldn't be helped though. His car was full; he was taking the office girls, who were also bidden to the junketing. I told him not to worry, I would make it somehow. By sheer chance I followed him through town centre, driving my first new Spitfire; I had collected it literally the day before. £666 ex works; sounds crazy now. The typists were incensed. Why hadn't I told them? The day was hot; they had been baked to a frazzle.

After that it was no surprise to have their erstwhile benefactor turn up in the studio. He would be leaving the company shortly, he announced. He told me at length about an offer he had received to work in New York. As he embroidered the fantasy, he crossed his legs and wagged a foot. I tried to keep my eyes averted. The sole of his shoe had become separated from the upper; I was fascinated by the opening and closing of the telltale gap. I happened to know he had a big family and a gambling problem; he was considerably in debt to the boss's son-in-law, who had become incensed one day and had unwisely opened his mouth. I wished him success, and resisted the temptation to hope that he would find a good cobbler in the Big Apple. Under the circumstances, it would have seemed less than worthy.

I seem to have led an oddly virtuous life. I never visited a strip show either, and for a long while never saw a blue movie. Though my virginity was spoiled in that respect by a friend in Waitrose-on-Thames. He was a curious man in many respects, who habitually described himself as the town's leading pseudo-intellectual and who managed by one means or another to stage a seemingly endless series of loss-making Shakespearean productions in the local theatre; there was an outrageous quality to his posing that I found perennially engaging. He was also a considerable film buff and a source of supply for blue movies, which he loaned with seeming freedom to anybody whose taste ran in that direction. With one exception, which he solemnly screened for me one evening. The girl involved was very beautiful, with dazzlingly long legs; she was his idol, a fantasy he acknowledged as cheerfully as the rest. I was intrigued in turn. Something vital seemed to hover at the edges of awareness, something denied by the crudeness of repeated images; the knees of the goddess being shoved irritably apart by a succession of extremely naked partners. So that's how folk behave, either on or off camera. What was in her mind though? What exactly was going through her head? My reaction was rather like Elagabalus in Alfred Duggan's classic evocation of the life and times of that strange Emperor. He became concerned for the well-being of a young prostitute hired for his delectation; and his aides had only chosen her because she bruised easily. They thought it would turn him on.

I glance at Lemady. As usual, to celebrate the arrival of summer weather she has anointed herself liberally with *Ambre Solaire*. It has had its customary effect; she has turned golden-brown, seemingly overnight. I repeat a libellous allegation that the preparation contains a skin dye. Also as usual, she denies it strenuously. "I just tan easily; I always have." Later, with the sun, her long hair will develop a wonderful complexity of tints; strands of brown, red-gold, near white. My observation of her is detailed and intense; a memory bank is building from which I am to draw, time and again. In celebration, not exploitation.

I turn off the main Bath Road, pull into the car park of a pub we favor. It's a handsome enough building; but there are many handsome pubs. Yet Lemady chose it at once, the first time we passed this way. And she was right. After a first-rate lunch we were invited to choose fruit for ourselves from a vast, overflowing bowl on the sideboard of the dining room; the first time I had ever known that happen, and very near the last. She has worked the oracle since, time after time, with equal success. I reckon to have a fair nose for a hostelry; but she is unerring. Finally I demand to know the secret. She looks haughty at first, murmers vaguely about vibes; finally she owns up. "I check for Rover cars outside. Farmers always know the best value." At heart, she is the ultimate pragmatist.

Perhaps most women are, perforce. They may be Mata Hari to their partners, Salome; but at the end of the day, who makes sure the loo paper doesn't run out?

With Lemady the two sides of her nature, the practical and the dreamily romantic, endlessly conflict. She shows me an article she once wrote, on Stonehenge. It's literate enough; unfortunately the dreamy side was allowed to prevail, to the detriment, finally, of basic facts. She has made the classic error; not all the stones were hauled from Prescelly. The great inner ring, the towering trilithons, were quarried from the sarsen sheet that once overlaid all Wiltshire.

"What's the matter? Don't you like it?"

Politeness wars with honesty. "Yes, of course. It's just...it's only a little thing...."

Her jaw has set. "Go on...."

I flounder. "It's the small stones round the edge that came from Wales. The Bluestones. They brought them to make the magic stronger. You could put it right, honestly. It would only take a moment...."

She snatches the typescript from me, in quiet fury. Her literary efforts are discontinued; for the duration, or so it seems. I end up feeling guilty. She has that knack.

Carried to excess, honesty can come to seem a species of vice. "Truth made naked without purpose is really a wanton," observes a John Wyndham character jauntily in *The Kraken Wakes*. Tennyson put it more soberly: "Lest one good custom should corrupt the world...." As a small boy I was habitually disbelieved. So I became skilled at constructing lies, owning up to things I hadn't done if I sensed it would make life easier. Now I have a pathological hatred of the process. The mechanism is clear enough; but it doesn't always help.

One of the TV channels offers a course in computing. Well, in for a penny, etc. The first programme, or should one say program, opens with an appropriately eerie shot of the Great Henge. The presenter appears. His shirt is cartwheel-striped, and his grin reminds me somehow of a trenching tool. "*Stonehenge* is a *computer*," he proclaims. It's my personal best time for reaching the off switch. Only four words in; and one of those was the indefinite article.

Later, a young man announces to me proudly that Stonehenge has been Decoded. They've even written a book to prove it. It's all mathematical; the stones are just there for markers.

"Fine. But if they were that smart, why not use the first rock that came to hand? The Plain was covered with them. Why drag all that junk from Wales?"

He looks thoughtful. "You've got a point. I don't think I'll bother with that book after all."

So I'm an old fuddy-duddy, fighting a hopeless rearguard action; like the Diffusionists rejecting the revised timescales of the tree-ring people. I'm fighting a rearguard action all right; but for common sense. I've even seen it claimed, with apparent seriousness, that the Bluestones were pushed to Wiltshire by glacial action. Ignoring small accidents of geography like the Avon Gorge. It's the urge to ram all concepts into a modern frame of thinking, whatever the cost to logic, that I really find bizarre.

A friend who drives for National Carriers detours his truck to find the Rollright Stones. When he gets back he looks thoughtful. "Three things I want to know. How old are they; who put them there; and why...."

He looks upset when I laugh. "I know they're stupid questions...."

"No, don't get me wrong. Go into any Common Room in the country, and say the same, and you'd start a right old punchup...."

He brightens. "You mean they don't know either? I thought it was all cut and dried...."

I felt the same, once, about the end of Roman Britain.

Elaine, my model for Maggie Blighe, deserts archaeology. "I was fed up with three month contracts. In any case, I'd never have got on."

"Why so?"

"When I didn't know what something was, I said so. That's no good. You've got to be positive; it doesn't really matter whether you're right or wrong.

Lemady is spooked by the Rollrights. She stares round her, at the disfigured shapes of the stones. Then she asks me to take her away. "They're like sex...."

Later, she qualifies the comment. "No. Sex is nice. They're like diseased sex...."

All right, so decode Lemady; then I'll think about the rest.

She buys a house, in the Market Place of what a friend is later to dub Waitrose-on-Thames. I have nothing but admiration for the excellent John Lewis Partnership; but the phrase still seems curiously apt. She sets to with a will. I help where I can; for the most part though, I stand back in awe. Within weeks, the place is transformed; complete to the bay trees each side of the freshly-painted front door. Toward the end of the process a friend visits, from a village a few miles upstream. I disliked her the first time we met; why should the socially superior always seem to have pointed noses? But Lemady rebuked my cynicism. If I took the trouble to get to know her, I would find she was really very sweet.

Coffee and biscuits are produced; and the friend goes into her act. Really expert snobs are never rude of course; it's their politeness that's designed to crush. She affects transports at the *tininess* of the tall, slender Town House. "My dear, how you managed to fit so much in I shall *never* know. I'm sure I never could. Those books in the sitting room, for instance. It's positively wall to *wall*; but when you look at it, I mean, it's *minute*. You've been so *clever*...."

Bedrooms, loo, kitchen, all come under the same remorseless hammer. Lemady's complexion darkens by degrees. Finally it's the turn of the garden. Agreed, it is tiny; but there she has worked her finest magic. She had the old walls pointed, and rewhitened; container roses make a vivid display, a leaden Cape Cod fisherboy casts his miniature line, a raised lawn is retained by a wall of Cotswold stone. Unbeknown, she has recreated the yard of a pub I know well in Dorset. There, fishing tackle hangs against similarly whitened brick; the artifacts make strange Signals, like the Tristram Hillier print I discovered in the basement of my art school, and got to know so well. But at sight of the place the gush of praise falters for the first time. "Oh.... Well of course, even you couldn't be expected to do anything with *that*...."

No. Only create wonder; but that is not for the herd.

Lemady's lips have set into a hard, sculpted line. It's an expression I've seen just once or twice before. Now, it would be a fool who braved her. Not that I have any wish to. My feelings are wholly of sympathy; that and anger at stupidity, small-mindedness. After the friend has left, we take another coffee in silence. I remember a story Lemady told me once; herself at school, a midnight feast, an arch enemy into whose bunk she had thoughtfully introduced thistles. When the expected tread came, in the corridor outside the dorm, the participants dived for their respective havens; the enemy lay mute on her bed of pain until the lights were clicked off, at which the fight began.

"Who won?"

"I did," says Lemady composedly. "I don't start things like that unless I'm prepared to see them through."

Shades of Molly Zero perhaps, my own much later heroine? Who is to prevent them? I for one have no wish to try.

Design of habitats has been an interest that has wandered through a lot of what I've done, from Libby Maynard's curious pad in my early book *The Inner Wheel* to the sculptor's even stranger garden in *Gráinne*, with its motif of the Piddling Nymph. They would probably make quite a list; but nobody would bother to compile it. The Nymph apart, there are few opportunities for prurient speculation. In a sense, Lemady was looking over my shoulder most of the time. She would by no means always approve of the results; but she would find them interesting.

Thoughts of Molly induce curious memories. One is of her birth. For all practical purposes, it took place on the train a mile or so from Waitrose-on-Thames. I had been to Town, to the offices of a major TV company, and had been left with a problem. This treatment I am required to write; what exactly can be done with it? The mysteriously-incarcerated men, one less in each episode, the shadowy watchers laying bets on who will vanish next; *The Prisoner* has already been made. Not only made, but repeated to exhaustion. I have to come up with something though; or I shall never hear the last of it from my agent of the time. Wingeing will be the order of the day; or GBH of the ear'ole, as a Brummie friend once memorably put it.

One thing seems certain. A previous brush with the world of film and TV production has taught me caution; I doubt there will be anything in it for me. This is a slow news week; it's time to stir up a few hicks from the sticks, but nothing more. Deadlines are like hanging though; they concentrate the mind wonderfully. And something is definitely there. But the last thing I want is for the putative producer, after rejecting the treatment, to turn round and say it was his idea anyway, I have merely written it up.

My station is almost in sight when the great notion dawns. Why not make the unknown people *girls*? That way, surely, I shall be bombproof.

Quick now. This has to be sorted; I can still save something from the day. A protagonist, that's what's needed; what can I call her? Recently, to her delight, my landlady succeeded in growing a tiny, delicate pansy. Its name is Irish Molly; its petals are a unique bronze-green. So I not only have a name; I have a nationality.

The thing is science-fictional already; so a number would seem to be indicated rather than a surname. Numbers though are not necessarily memorable; in themselves at least. Except one. Molly, the ultimate Zero. For a time, that was what I thought she had become.

I'm recalled to London, by a sorrowful producer. What I produced bears no relation to what had been discussed; it's no use to him at all. In fact, apart from the gender change, it bears every relation. Cheap to do as well; no crowd scenes, precious few exteriors. He has another piece of bad news though. The company is very hard up this week; they can't afford a kill fee.

I bear the revelation, like Kipling's immortal Sleary, with a chastened, holy joy. If I happened to be in the Screenwriters' Guild I could get my money fast enough; just threaten to blow the whistle. As a matter of fact I'm not, though I did once have the chance to join. It's another casual assumption the great man has made; hicks from the sticks don't know about that sort of thing.

"You mean it's nothing to do with your idea at all?"

"No, nothing whatever. Nothing I can do with this."

"Right. You may have noticed it's written in the form of an sf novella. I shall sell it as one." By sheer chance, I have already had an inquiry.

He has the cheek to look surprised. Taken aback might be a better description. I'm quite sure somewhere, Lemady is laughing.

As a matter of fact it's just as well I wasn't in a position to approach the Guild. I'd have got it in the neck from them as well. I find out later, from a friend who processes TV contracts, the thing is over length for a treatment; there are strict rules laid down for that too.

There has to be a framework for such things of course; or the originator gets walked on every time. Whether from sheer indifference or the need to prove superiority by putting down everyone in sight I've never been too sure; though over the years I have been forced increasingly to suspect the latter. During my own TV stint, my employer required that I vacate my studio when clients visited from Town; in my absence he passed my work off as his own. He came spectacularly unstuck once. I was chatting to the secretary when a roar of rage emerged from the inner sanctum. My presence was required, at once.

The affair was readily enough explained. The client had asked, with calculated innocence, what typeface had been used for the title sequence that had been prepared; he wanted to match it if possible in the advertising. Now he sits in state in the little Viewing theatre, his presenter, an elegant ex-model, at his side. "Ah," he says urbanely, "we meet the man who actually did the job...." Then after a pause, "What's the matter? Aren't your employees allowed to drink coffee in work time?"

I'm slung a couple of tickets for the first transmission of the new show. My Master has lost interest. The presenter has become, for him, "a bloody cow with a leg at each corner"; so it seems in the interim his charm has failed on her. I take a gift with me. She had fallen for a visual I had done, thumbtacked to the display board in Reception. Fair enough; I had long ago fallen conclusively for her. I prepare finished art, and frame it; in the firm's time, and for the firm's good name. It's a curious situation; "piquant" is an adjective that flits across the mind.

The situation had been piquant from the start of course. The producer might not be a very nice guy, but he's nobody's fool. He knew as well as I did the typography of the *Radio Times* isn't a moveable feast. The initial question was designed to bring an already patent fact fully into the open.

Despite the clanger, or maybe because of it, my employer's ego becomes even more obtrusive. I would have crawled into a hole, had I been put down so conclusively, and pulled the hole in after me; but then, I would never have got myself into that sort of situation in the first place. It wouldn't have been possible; my mind doesn't work that way. It's like one of the Buddha's unanswerable riddles; if there is no answer, there cannot be a question. It's best to turn away, and tiptoe quietly off.

Riding on other people's backs, or trying to, has always been a source of puzzlement to me. I would take no pleasure in the process; rather, it would irritate. It would remind me of my own shortcomings. I'm obviously in a minority though, because it seems a common human trait. "Other Buggers' Efforts" is a well enough known variation on the title O.B.E. Doubtless many earn the honor fairly; but the jibe did not come about wholly by chance.

A fair while later I decide it's time to develop Molly's story. I had already built a point into the novella where the thing could be opened out to become a saga. For a variety of reasons, I stop for six months with the job partially complete. A lot happens in the interval, including a trip to Ireland. I used to offer ten cent cigars to anybody who could spot the join; but the challenge was never taken up, so I let it lapse. There are hiccups and setbacks of course; there always are. The first and biggest is that the tense I chose merely to give the original some sort of life, the second singular, has to be maintained. Changing it would be like changing horses in midstream; it can't be done, gracefully at least. Though the strange viewpoint is not without advantages. The effect produced seems both intimate and remote at the same time. The virtues don't seem to extend to the bulk of the reviewers. "It appears to me," says an acquaintance judicially, "that it's all right to be unconventional, as long as you're unconventional along conventional lines." I agree. He's an unpleasant fellow; but for once he has a point.

The fact that the thing has promotion in accordance with its title, and that the English paperback looks like some sort of manual of World War Two fighting aircraft, might have a slight bearing; but that's typical of authors. If a book doesn't sell, it's their own fault; it can never be the publishers. After all, they're experts.

Actually, I have an image of Molly lined up. I wouldn't be allowed to influence production, naturally; authors know nothing about artwork. But I happen to know a beautiful Irish blonde. She's in her first year at Oxford; just about Molly's age. And there's a futuristic plaza in Reading that would make a perfect backdrop. My colleague would take the shots; I could smuggle them to the artist commissioned to do the job, and the problem would be solved. All we really need is a trench coat.

The model's father—the same legal eagle, as it happens, who advised me on treatment lengths—invites me to dinner. I put the idea to him. He hesitates. "Yes," he says after a moment. "Sounds all right...."

I'm puzzled. He's known me long enough, he knows I'm straight. We listen to vintage Peggy Lee records for a while; then he produces a Kodak wallet. "I didn't show you my holiday snaps, did I?"

The puzzlement deepens. He isn't the sort of man to do that either.

The mystery is rapidly explained. My ghostly Molly has cropped her shoulder-length mane into a sort of spiky semi-punk. My friend watches my face. "What do you think she looks like?"

"A tired Earley housewife."

"Then you tell her so. I daren't; I'm only her father...."

There are such things as wigs of course; these days they're pretty good. But family politics would obviously preclude. So the idea is stillborn, like many another. You can't win 'em all though. Molly finds out the hard way; I knew already.

Prior to the typescript going to the printers, a production secretary rings up with a couple of small queries. I've met her the odd time; leastways I think I have. The points are rapidly resolved. I'm about to hang up when she speaks again. "Can I make a comment?"

"Of course. Feel free."

"I'd like to say how much I enjoyed working with this book. Good luck with it."

Keith Roberts

"Thank you. Praise from a professional. That's worth a lot to me."

"Sorry?"

"I write a hundred thousand words about an attractive young woman. And another says she likes it. I can't have gone all that far wrong."

It's true of course. It means more than all the reviewers standing in a line and cheering; or baying, which turns out to be the case.

When a French edition of *Molly Zero* becomes due, a fresh problem suggests itself. In English, with its decayed declensions, it did not arise; "you" is both singular and plural. But in French? I am curious enough to write to Michel Demuth, the series editor for Calmann-Levy. Will it be the formal *vous*; or *tu*, used to children, loved ones, and, I understand, servants by the high-born? His answer is memorable. "I see no reason why the entity who speaks to Molly throughout should not use an intimate form." I am delighted. It reflects my own thoughts; it makes a point that could not have been made in my native tongue.

I'm approached by a young man currently doing a course of sf appreciation; *Molly Zero* has been chosen as a text. He asks particularly about the tense; so I explain how it came about. It seems he becomes progressively less happy. But the horse's mouth is often unsatisfying. Much better to stay at a distance, and guess. That way one preserves the glamour.

Unexpectedly, a cover flat arrives. I wonder why it has been sent to me. Later I'm telephoned from the publishers. I say what the caller basically wants to hear. What shelf would the finished product be displayed on? Romantic fiction seems the obvious answer; except that M & B covers are prettier, it would lose by comparison. She agrees, sadly. The job must be recommissioned. She wouldn't trust the eyes God allegedly gave her, or the thing behind that is popularly called a brain; but somewhere a still, small voice had whispered all was not well. She wanted it confirmed; so us backstreet hacks have our uses after all.

Inescapably, the incident gives rise to a couple of thoughts. I happen to know the current rate for color separations. Add that to the very modest fee paid to the artist, double both; and they have coughed several times what they gave for reuse of the text. In which there must be a moral, though I hesitate to draw it. "The trouble they go to," observed a colleague once, viewing a not dissimilar effort, "to get things wrong...."

16

It isn't the illustrator's fault. I am to chat with him, some time later; he calls me, very conscientously, to ask if I can give him any idea what the Cody strings of my later book *Kiteworld* look like.

"I can do better than that. I'll send you down some stats of the working drawings."

"Good Lord. You mean they were real?"

"They certainly were. Cody flogged the design to the British Government just before World War One. Only hydrogen balloons came along instead, so manlifting kites were never used. They still fly them in the States though. Here as well, sometimes. That wasn't Buffalo Bill by the way; it was Samuel, who started Farnborough. Mention him to an RAF man, they usually get the prayer mat out."

We laugh, a little sadly, about the *Molly Zero* fiasco. I'd been ahead of the problem anyway. He didn't have a model; and he couldn't afford to hire. It would have cost more than the job was paying him. So he had to make do. Aerial views, machinery; you can get by. With the human figure, never. Da Vinci couldn't, or any artist born. No doubt certain readers would be disappointed. What? You mean it isn't original, we don't make it up out of our heads? To the simple-minded though, all things are simple; or equally confusing.

The first time I heard the phrase "visual illiteracy" I was confused myself. Then I realized how apposite it was. The condition itself had always puzzled me. Reading, after all, requires that one accesses a code; I can quite see circumstances arising where for one reason or another this is not possible. For the rest though, all you have to do is open your eyes and look. Nonetheless, it's a standard problem with the English; presumably other nations too. Publishers have their full share; and sadly, authors. Leastways, the exceptions shine by contrast. It always troubled me that those who pride themselves on creating images for others should be so wanting in the area themselves.

So why complain about the packaging? If people can't see what they're looking at, it shouldn't matter what's done for a wrapper. There are two answers to this. Bad drawings give me a pain; it's a natural instinct to avoid unpleasant stimulus. The second is more general. A buyer for a London bookshop doubles his order at sight of a cover produced by my colleague. It's a striking offering. The girl's brooding face; the hard black and white of the treatment, so at contrast with the blaze of color on the shelves round about. The buyer hasn't opened the book; but he believes it will sell.

So, there are returns later on; there always are. That isn't the point. Another set of values is involved. They go under a collective head: design. Or graphics, if you have to have a buzzword. The name of the game is getting the product into the punter's hand; that holds as true for books as breakfast cereals.

For a time I felt I should adopt the pompous and meaningless phrase "graphic designer" myself. I had always had a job describing what I did; I thought it might cut down on explanations. "Commercial artist" is no use; it always produces the same response.

"Oh. You do cards for shop windows."

"No. They're ticket writers. It's quite different...."

I'm cured at a stroke. Like one of the single strokes ticket writers use.

I'm traveling from London to Wiltshire on the coach. Usually it's an enjoyable trip; once clear of the environs of Victoria at least. On this occasion a sudden heatwave has made life hard all round. In response, the air conditioning above the seats has failed.

A late passenger appears. He's a bulky, unprepossessing lout, hung about with guitars and assorted electronic gear. The driver is uncompromising. Either that junk goes in the boot, or he doesn't board.

The vision protests. It's worth a lot of money; what would happen if he lost it?

The driver is unrelenting. "I'd say good. We might all get some peace...." But it is not to be. The newcomer attaches himself to a schoolgirl, traveling unaccompanied. He begins a recital of past triumphs, in the musical field and others. She proves a good audience. She gazes at him, it seems with admiration. Her jaw sags progressively; her face, in Stella Gibbons's glowing phrase, has all the wild freshness of a newly born leveret.

An hour or so into the journey she produces a newspaper. Her companion is obviously destined for great things; he would find his horoscope interesting. But he waves the paper away in lordly fashion. She must impart the information to him; he cannot read. He has no need to; he is a graphic designer.

When I leave the coach, I tip the driver. He has earned it. He had to put up with just as much as me; and he was working as well. I also make a mental note. The term always irritated; but now I shall certainly not use it again. I have an *aide-memoire*.

The American images for *Kiteworld* are hilarious. A hot air rig blasts its output into a clear blue sky. "Well, they use those things for balloons an' stuff, don't they?" The paperback offering is even more striking; a line of objects like flying Rotolators, mysteriously made airborne. "Well, hell, it's ski-fi, ain't it? So give it a ski-fi cover...."

In themselves these things are not of critical importance; nit-picking is not one of my preferred sports. What is significant is that they reveal the level of thought that was involved. It didn't exist.

Prior to my Guest of Honor stint at Birmingham, I am approached by one of the multifarious directors of Kerosina. Wouldn't it be a good idea to fly a Cody rig from the forecourt of the hotel? It would be jolly good promotion for the book.

"I'm sure it would be. There's just one thing. We're underneath the airport flight path, just where they let down. The Airways Authority might have something to say."

"Ah. Yes. I suppose you *might* have a point...."

Lemady would never have come out with such a gem. An old fashioned quality seems called for. In my young days, we would have called it gumption.

I wonder sometimes if Lemady ever saw the *Kiteworld* opus. And what she made of it if she did. Matters aerial would have a strong appeal for her. After all, she always declared she would learn to fly herself one day. But she would leave it till she reached the age of eighty; it would seem more worth doing then. I have confidence. Her God will protect her; or her Goddess.

II.

Lemady and I are at the gateway to the Cotswolds. Or so I've heard it called. Though I suppose that depends which direction you're going in.

Certainly we're on the tourist track; a well worn pathway for Americans and others. Signs of it abound; the town is home to one of the most concentrated collections of antique shops I have seen. They stretch on down the long main street, disappear in distance. As yet I have not found an acceptable collective noun. An elderly friend always insisted such things alliterate; but my offerings seldom met with approval. Save one, coined after what had apparently been a singularly disastrous day for the racing enthusiasts. "How about a Beatitude of Bookies?" My friend, a Catholic of the old school, smiled seraphically. I had touched his wavelength.

Lemady could never resist an antique shop; or a rich man's Woolworths, depending on one's viewpoint. After a morning of hectic browsing, mine is becoming distinctly jaded. I want something to eat; and a glass of ale to wash it down.

"Just one more; then we'll go, honestly. There's still plenty of time." I sigh, and give in. Time, after all, is notoriously subjective. My illustration tutor always used to say there's as much of it as you want. If you run out, just make some more. I have news for him. There isn't, and you can't. The lunchtime session is just about over.

As the centerpiece of its window display, the last port of call features a ferociously-priced set of boxwood gaming pieces. NINE MEN'S MORRIS, proclaims a hand-scrawled showcard. AS DE-SCRIBED IN SHAKESPEARE'S "A MIDSUMMER NIGHT'S DREAM." For me, it's almost the last straw.

We enter. The dulcet tones of the bell seem to take ages to die away. A lady emerges from the genteel gloom. She looks me up and down, decides I'm not really quality and turns to Lemady. She's right of course; it's just that it's rude to make it so plain.

"Can I help you, madam?"

"Yes. We were interested in the Nine Men's Morris."

Lemady might be, but I'm not. Not at that sort of price anyway.

The lady purrs contentedly. "Yes. Beautiful, isn't it? It's as described by Shakespeare you know. In 'A Midsummer Night's Dream'."

"It isn't..."

The lady collects herself and tries again. She ignores me stoically. "As I was saying, madam; it's as he described it in 'A Midsummer Night's Dream'."

"*It isn't...*"

By the third time round I can contain myself no longer. Not that I've made much of a fist of it up to now. "The lines you're groping for are Titania to Oberon, Act Two, Scene One. 'The Nine Men's Morris is fill'd up with mud, and the quaint mazes in the wanton green, for lack of tread are indistinguishable.' Which hardly sounds like a bloody board game..." The bell announces my departure, with a quiet vehemence of its own.

I wait by the car. After a minute or so Lemady appears. Her face seems stiffly composed. I brace myself for the coming storm.

"Are you all right?"

"Yes, thank you."

"Shall we carry on?"

"Yes, of course."

She makes a sort of choking sound. I glance at her sharply. Her shoulders are shaking. I realize she is laughing.

She wipes her eyes, composes herself. "It was very wrong of you. But it was very funny. I didn't know where to put my face; I was getting giggles in my cheeks."

"I know it was. I was just fed up. What did the old trout do?"

"Nothing. There wasn't much *to* do, was there? She opened her mouth and shut it a couple of times; that was about all."

"There are two sorts of Nine Men's Morris, you see," I venture. "It started out as a sort of field game."

"Forget it," says Lemady crisply. "Just drive on."

We are touring, in Dorset. Lemady has chosen the route. She is directing me; she won't say where we're heading.

The Bockhamptons draw remorselessly nearer. I slow down. "I am *not* going to Hardy's Birthplace."

"Well, I want to. It looks interesting."

I give in. It's getting to be a habit. We pull up, walk toward the old thatched cottage. The garden is ablaze with hollyhocks. It's a fitting subject for a postcard; or a jigsaw puzzle. I say as much, maliciously. Lemady has a hangup about such things. Somebody told her once, jigsaw addicts have sex problems. Maybe the dislike predated the remark; but she certainly avoids them scrupulously now.

The curator appears. She is small, and spiky-nosed. We shall have to wait until a sufficient group has assembled. But I suppose that's fair enough. This is a National Trust property; she shows folk round in lieu of rent. There's no bonus for extra tours.

We are admitted finally. By that time my mood has definitely deproved. The wait seemed endless; and the afternoon got hotter as it wore on. We are met by a rich stench of dog. It hardly improves matters.

The curator smiles at me toothily. "Are you a Hardy enthusiast?"

"*No....*"

Well, she asked a straight question; and it was answered honestly. It's hardly a good start though. The old curse strikes again.

The inside of the place is plain, and somewhat cramped. It has nothing to do with Hardy; but then, it never did. Max Gate was the house he built; the place somebody once said needed a Ghost Course, where others merely need protection from rising damp.

"That's a complete set of his novels. It has nothing to do with him; it belongs to us."

That figures.

"The furniture in this room is ours as well. We brought it with us. In fact, all the furniture down here. It has nothing to do with Hardy."

We are shown a tiny aperture in one of the thick walls. But that has nothing to do with Hardy either; it was where his father used to pay his men. Later I am to see just such a thing in the film they made of *Far from the Madding Crowd*. It causes an odd pang.

We trail upstairs. The litany is resumed. "That bed has nothing to do with Hardy. Also, the chairs in this room. They're ours...."

Bully for you, lady. I don't go much on your taste though.

We collect finally round a tall Victorian writing desk. The group gazes at it with a species of faint hope.

"That's ours of course; it has nothing to do with Hardy. And we don't know if he wrote any of his novels here. But we thought, *if* he did, and *if* he owned a desk like that, he *might* have put it there...." Our informant indicates a rough trapdoor, set at head height in the wall. "That leads to a sort of attic. It wasn't there in Hardy's time; so we can be sure of one thing. He wouldn't have been in a draught...."

"My God," I say in a heartfelt voice. "That's a relief...."

Downstairs again, a framed map of Dorset takes my eye. On it in red are inked the great man's alternate place names. Completing the list seems to be the life preoccupation of most Hardy buffs. Never mind the quality, feel the width.

The curator looks proud. "My husband and I did that. You'll find they're all there...."

"They're not."

"What?"

"He used two names for Corfe. I can see Coombe Castle; where's the other one?"

Lemady opens the door. "Thank you *so* much," she says. "It's been very interesting." She doesn't exactly wag her thumb at me; but she might just as well have. For once I don't argue. I have a strong feeling I've already pushed it far enough.

Knocking everybody else is an unenviable trait of most writers. But I get little feel of Dorset, either past or present, from Hardy, hailed though he is as the great chronicler of the county. A rural atmosphere of sorts perhaps; but for that I frankly prefer *Cold Comfort Farm*. A real place name once on a time, in Northamptonshire; in her zaniness, Stella Gibbons strangely got closer to the mark. Also, she created my second-favorite heroine (the all-out winner is Alice). I treasure Flora's remark after she has given a half-witted bumpkin some elementary contraceptive instruction. The girl's eyes widen.
"That be flyin' in the face of Nature...."
"Yes," says Flora firmly. "That's right...."
For me Hardy is an infuriating writer. Much of his output I find frankly turgid; I'm glad he wasn't in vogue when I was at school, it might just have put me off reading for good. *Jude the Obscure* was too obscure for me, while I never even got as far as Ethelberta's hand. The Introduction was enough; half a dozen pages explaining that the book was a comedy, and exhorting the reader to laugh, succeeded in subduing my enthusiasm. Occasionally though, unforgettable moments scorch through the verbal fog. In *Tess*, the horse groans in blackness as the splintered cart-shaft pierces its heart; Blackmore, whose most telling passages are often built from sound effects, could scarcely have done better. While I can never forget the "fallen woman" of the poem, mournfully displaying her finery, and mocking her respectable, horny-handed friend. Briefly, Hardy touches the very essence of femaleness; it's a pity he couldn't do it more often.

At a local pub Lemady and I use, we have offended the resident pundit. Leastways, I have. How, I'm not too sure; but he seems to consider himself some sort of literary lion, maybe the sound of a typer from the little van I use at the back offends him. I said nothing about what I was doing; but it seems I had no need. If I dare show my nose, it's certain the needling will start. After a day-long stint, all I want is a quiet beer; but it is never allowed. "*Now* I must be silent; *now* we have a *real* writer among us...."
Oh, for Christ's sake. Why doesn't he scab up and drop off?
He is also a Hardy addict. Or so he claims. I observe that his main virtue as a poet was that he couldn't scan. Unfair, and wholly untrue; but at least it produces a change of tack. Our friend re-engages on his other great love: travel. He must be the most knowledgeable person in the business; certainly wherever you happen to mention, he

invariably knows it well. Lemady hints at an affection for the Isle of Purbeck.

"Ah, Purbeck. Now you're talking of course. Delightful, totally delightful. So pretty...."

She brightens. "Yes. If you turn left off the road, anywhere between Wareham and Corfe. All those little villages...."

But there's nothing between Wareham and Corfe. Just the heath, and saltings. It's the wildest and most desolate part of a fairly desolate area. "I—" I say. "Ouch." She has kicked my ankle under the table, with remarkable accuracy. "What are they called?" she asks, wide-eyed. "I can't remember any of them. I was always hopeless at names...."

Her victim presses a hand to his forehead. "Don't help me," he says. "Don't help me, it'll come. Upper and Lower something, I'm almost sure. Yes, it's coming back. I can see them as clearly as if I was there...."

I'm sitting a little unhappily in a pub in Waitrose-on-Thames. It's a nice sunny morning, and I'd come out for a nice quiet ale. But it was not to be. I've been buttonholed by a gentleman in blazer and white slacks; his head is adorned with what Kipling once called a spardecked yachting cap. He's expounding on the joys of certain French villages, in each of which apparently Picasso once established a studio. Obviously I must know them well. Something *sur Mer*, *Église sur* something else; and oh heavens, what *is* that one with the line of poplars on the approach? You round the bend of the road, and there it is spread out. A picture, an absolute picture; I *must* know it. The name's on the tip of his tongue.

I'm conscious a frown has started to form. I haven't the faintest idea what he's talking about, even if he has; getting me to admit it is going to be the highlight of his day. But I can't get rid of him either, not without being rude; so it's a no-win situation. That's the way his sort invariably play it though. What I really need is for Lemady to materialize suddenly; but that's not going to happen, she's away for the weekend.

My persecutor is anxious to help; or hasten the *débâcle*. I'm looking troubled; what seems to be the problem?

Suddenly there's no problem; no problem at all. I favor him with a broad smile.

"Who's Picasso?"

I suppose he could do a number of things. Faint, hang one on me; all sorts. What he actually does is set his glass down with a species of careful precision, turn on his heel and walk out without another word. Pity. And I wasn't rude either; just asked a civil question.

Fantasy construction is always an interesting process. Certainly it's one many folk indulge in. Most folk, I sometimes think. The difference with me is that I later spend a few weeks hammering a typewriter, or liaising with a print shop manager. But that's my artistic side coming out; I will insist on sullying the thing with nasty practicalities.

A studio manager I suffered once undertook to sum up the artistic attitude. "When folk look at an egg," he said sententiously, "they see different things. A farmer sees profit, a housewife sees a breakfast; an artist sees an egg." There's a pleasing, positively Oriental pragmatism there; it's a pity he couldn't apply his clearsightedness to his own affairs. In Germany in 1945, he drank water from a standpipe among ruins and gave himself a touch of typhus; he was invalided home, a hero in hospital blue, and never did a hand's turn afterward. The War had ruined him; he had acquired his psychological prop. Now, on the desk in front of him sit three small pots of poster color; red, yellow, and blue. You can have whichever you like; but don't expect him to *mix* them. That takes effort; and he has done his bit.

Interestingly, he is not a happy man. Quite the contrary; he is morose to a degree. Boredom has succeeded the onset of pathological idleness; but the pattern is too strong to break. So often it seems, the end result of mental states is polar to what might be expected.

I'm sitting in a pub in Waitrose-on-Thames. It's nearly midnight; but the company, with the connivance of the landlord, is still whooping it up. In their enthusiasm, the revellers have forgotten to shoot the bolt on the street door. It opens suddenly, and complete silence falls. But it isn't the Law. Instead, a Dickensian vision appears. It's thin and bony; it clutches a dressing gown round itself and its head is adorned, incredibly, with curling papers. It wags its thumb at the street; the very gesture Lemady would never ever make. The husband, a small, loquacious butcher from the shop across the road, sets his cup down and slinks out without a word. He's never the same man; nor will he be, until he finds another watering-hole. One in which his shame is not known.

His deflation is striking enough; but what rivets me is the expression on the wife's face. There's rage there certainly, and bitterness; but also there's profound misery. "This isn't how things should be," she seems to be saying. "Somehow, it's not what life should be about." She hasn't analyzed, perhaps she can't; but in any case there's nothing to be done. She has him under her thumb, that much is painfully plain; but she remains unsatisfied. She despises him for his submissiveness, and through him herself; so the failure, and the guilt, are shared.

When I was still a student, my loving mother suddenly saw fit to give me the benefit of her experience; experience, as it happened, she didn't possess. "When you marry," she said judicially, "Assuming you ever do, choose a plain woman. They're much less trouble...." I looked at her in horror. I would never marry, somehow I already knew; though the reasons hadn't been analyzed, at that time anyway. But that wasn't the point. What is a plain woman? Come to that, what's a pretty one? It's something that grows from inside, it's compounded of a host of factors. You can't use a tape measure on it, or lay down rules like the Hollywood moguls of old; line of lips not to extend beyond centres of eyes, and so on and on. That way, ultimately, lies madness; while the end result of my mother's thinking, or lack of it, is the sort of horror I witness in the doorway of that literally benighted boozer.

I watch a ballet version of *The Taming of the Shrew*. I develop a strong dislike of the girl dancing the lead. A Continental housewife, if I ever saw one; spiky, arrogant, using her elbows to force her way to the front of the shop. Later, her psychic destruction begins. Her feet drag, her shoulders droop. I feel corresponding sympathy. She is very lovely; but this shouldn't happen to anybody.

I realize, belatedly, she's acting. She was from the start. This is body language; and it fooled me. As it always can. By the end of the piece, she is radiant. Before, she was the unhappiest of souls; now she is in balance. The possibility of a relationship has at least emerged. It's a new viewpoint on Shakespeare's seemingly vicious epic. Far removed perhaps from the received wisdom of the late twentieth century; but a viewpoint nonetheless. Certainly the more raucous of our Women's Libbers would never grasp it. They wouldn't try; or perhaps, again, they couldn't. Balance is the key; the Greek ideal, moderation in all things. If it can be achieved of course; there, so often, is the rub.

I'm chatting to a couple of young visitors to Waitrose-on-Thames. The girl is comely and vivacious. She tells me she comes from Staines, and that she's a schoolteacher. "Only primary," she adds after a pause.

I happen to know Staines, just a bit. The old part anyway, courtesy of my colleague. The gracious square in the middle, the big pub on the river. While as for primary teaching.... "You have these kids at the most important time. Age of Reason and all that. When they leave you, their characters are formed. Don't do yourself down like that; you're vital...."

We get onto the subject of Women's Lib. The boyfriend groans. "Don't start her off on that. You'll be here all night...."

On the contrary, she is brisk and informative. I didn't know for instance the extent of GLC funding for some of the more belligerent publishing outfits currently springing up.

The first Kaeti series is already forming. "I'm working on some female-oriented stuff at the moment actually. I was wondering about trying it out on one of them."

She considers. "This heroine of yours. Is she shown beating men at every turn, physically, mentally, the lot?"

"Good lord, no. She has a hell of a time; sexual harassment, the lot."

My informant shakes her head. "Don't bother. They'd throw it at the wall."

"Does she really have to have Stars and Stripes on her knickers? Is it honestly as crude as that?"

"Yes...."

Oh well; I asked, and I was answered. So that's another avenue closed. Not, to be frank, that I'd had a sight of faith in it. Later I see some of the artwork the sorority produce, and develop even less.

"Biffering" is a new phrase to me. I find it's quite a widespread sport. It consists of male writers sending material in under pseudonym, to try and fool their newly-established Better Halves. One of the noisiest of the self-styled Amazons is particularly contemptuous of it; she can detect the work of a mere male, she proclaims, in a couple of sentences.

I feel faintly annoyed. For some time now she has been running ads asking for material; in big ink, as a Swiss acquaintance once put it. Only work by females will be considered. It drives a cart and horses through the Sex Discrimination Act of course, though nobody seems particularly concerned. This is different though. Apart from the absurdity of the claim, writing is a hard enough craft without things being complicated by unnecessary politics, sexual or any other sort. I take down one of the new Kaeti stories, consider it. It's one time I really feel the lack of a word processor. A couple of Kaeti pieces have already appeared in print, so the name will have to be changed. If I owned such a machine, presumably I could instruct it to search the text and make the necessary alterations. As it is, the job will have to be done by hand.

Presentation of the typescript is an important part of the operation. It purports to be written by a nervous beginner, one Richenda Steuart; a name that should ring alarm bells even if all else fails. I decide Richenda wouldn't use a folder; first-time authors don't. Not as a rule anyway. I should know; I handled enough amateur manuscripts during my time on *Science Fantasy* and *Impulse*. I pack the sheets into an A5 envelope instead, use a friend's P.O. box for a return address. Lastly comes the covering letter. I'm quite pleased with the end result. It slops over by just the right amount; it explains, irrelevantly, that Richenda has just moved to the area, after a hinted-at traumatic experience (let down by a *man*, almost certainly) and apologizes fulsomely for troubling such a busy person. It ends by begging any advice she feels able to give; the correspondent is desperate to justify her sad life by getting into print. A woman friend obligingly signs it for me; a female hand is a vital final touch. I'm really beginning to think I missed my vocation; I should have been in counter-espionage, or something of the sort.

The result is highly gratifying. Leastways, it seems to me to prove a point. They've closed the list on the story collection the editrix has been touting for, which I knew anyway; but she is most impressed by Richenda's work and feels she might well have a future in writing. Has she ever considered a *novel*? Though a female agent of my acquaintance (leastways, I believe her biologically to be of that persuasion) is unimpressed. It was only a short story after all; had it been a full length piece, they'd have detected the fraud within the statutory limit. Which again seems to make a point. It's fatiguing to use more than one brain cell at a time; so the exponents of mental austerity will always win. They can carry on burbling more or less indefinitely.

Typically, my legal friend has the final word. Out of curiosity I ask him what my position would have been had I written a novel as Richenda, sold it and succeeded in pocketing the advance. He considers gravely before delivering his verdict. "I think you would have been guilty of a fundamental deception...."

I have to withdraw some funds from my local Building Society. I'm shown into the manager's office. A girl faces me across the desk. She is neat and attractive, like the counter staff. Whoever chooses them has a good eye. I ask if all the personnel at the branch are female.

"As it happens, yes. At the moment anyway. Do you object?"

"Heavens, no. Quite the reverse. It was just a thought."

She waits.

"All this Women's Lib stuff. They did a lot of good at the start. But all they seem to do now is shout. Folk like you make your own way. You probably always could."

"Yes," she says. "Rather my thoughts. Now, how can I help you?"

Something like a flour bag crosses my mind. They throw them at the judges at beauty competitions. For the sake of fairness they should throw them at the contestants too. After all, it's their own sex they are letting down. They choose to parade themselves; the judges, so-called, are an irrelevance.

Nonetheless, I would like to have the choosing of a panel. I would select a sculptor, a gynecologist, and someone like Lemady.

There wouldn't be a showbiz personality in sight. The results might be quite interesting.

For once, I see the so-called generation gap actually operate. The younger daughter of a publican friend is being pressured by her mother. She wants her to go in for the beauty contest at the local agricultural show. "You don't realize," she says. "If you entered, you'd probably win...."

"'Course I'd bloody win," says the girl, exasperated. "But I just don't care. Got it?"

I buy her a drink, and we withdraw a little. She lights a cigarette. "I know I was a bit rude. But Mum's been going on about it for days." She glances at me. "You understand though, don't you?"

"I think so. But there's another thing. You might not have won, you know. Should have, goes without saying. But think of the sort of goons they get to do the judging."

She glances round her. "Yeah, I know. That would have really got me mad. It don't do to go on about that sort of thing though, does it?"

"I'm glad that happened," says Lemady cheerfully, after one of our infrequent rows.

"Why so?"

She looks serene. "Because it's so nice making up. We must do it again sometime." At that point perhaps, she's not a million miles away from the Shirtwaisters, the mystic band of women created by Gráinne, my TV newscaster turned Buddhist priest. Hers is a mind that looks at things straight on. For her, the so-called rough and smooth aren't polar; they are sides of the same coin. Well, most of the time.

* * * * * *

There's a certain brand of fiction in which women are likened persistently to cats. I love both species dearly but the simile has never appealed. Cats are chinless, four-legged and have fur; women are bipedal, have chins and don't. Maybe though any similarity is more psychological. Cats for the most part are the most self-possessed of animals; but if the unexpected happens, they're quite likely to throw a wobbly.

Lemady and I are spending the weekend in Dorset. We've lunched at a pub we both favor; outside, an elderly donkey peers morosely from the paddock. She instantly makes a beeline for it. "Oh, look. He's beautiful...."

That's the last adjective I would use. The creature is walleyed and potbellied; it has teeth like tombstones, while it looks as if every moth in creation has made a hearty meal from its coat. Nonetheless she begins to make a fuss of it, with appropriate billing and cooing noises.

The idyll is abruptly interrupted. She is sporting a raffia shoulder bag, one of the season's musts. The donkey clamps its teeth on it and begins to ingest it, to the accompaniment of smashing and tinkling from the innumerable bottles and jars of lotion she seems to find vital for the support of life. Instantly, a shrill scream arises. "Keith, *do* something!"

But I'm already doing something; I'm lying flat on a convenient grassy bank, and kicking my heels. What else could reasonably be expected of me?

All women pack a wallop of course, when sufficiently riled or when circumstances demand; but at five eleven, I would imagine Lemady packs more than most. She winds herself up and delivers the benighted animal such a tremendous punch on the nose it has to let go to sneeze. She snatches the erstwhile fashion accessory away. It looks distinctly the worse for wear. One side has extended gungily a foot or more; had it been an amoeba, I would have said it had developed a pseudopod. Arrived back at the campsite, it is conveyed tightlipped to the dustbin.

Sunday evening arrives. We pack for home, as regretfully as ever. A couple of miles from Corfe, I see a donkey peering over a gate.

It's no use. Try as I may, I can't keep my tongue between my teeth.

"Oh look, there's an old donk. Do you want to stop and make a fuss of him?"

I've heard of looks that stick six inches out of one's back. It's a wonder the glare I receive doesn't pass through me and burn holes in the side of the car. Donkeys cease to be a conversational topic between us; and she never makes a fuss of one again, in my presence at least. Who knows; perhaps her addiction was finally cured. Poor lady though; I really shouldn't have laughed quite so much.

III.

The odd *contretemps* is less amusing. Initially at least. Lemady sits in a field. Behind her is a Snow White cottage, twisty-chimneyed. The evening is fine and sunny; a pale glower over the hills hints at the nearness of the sea. Birds sing from a little spinney; but misery sits on her like a cloud. We had decided on a weekend camp on Purbeck; the magic person must come to know the magic place. At her request, I left all arrangements to her; and inexplicably, she didn't pack the pegs.

She beats her fists on the grass. It's sheer rage at herself. Then her shoulders droop; she just looks plain scared. I'm reminded, startlingly, of *Ice Cold in Alex*; a fine film made from an equally memorable book. They've wound the ambulance painfully to the top of a massive dune; and Nurse Murdoch omits to set the brake. Her reaction is exactly the same.

"What shall we do?" says Lemady helplessly. "What shall we do...."

"That's easy. Go back for them. We can't buy any down here; the shops will be shut by now."

"But you can't," she wails. "You can't. All that way...." Panic threatens to set in. "I don't want to go to a hotel. I can't...."

"That's all right. I don't want to go to a hotel either." I light a pipe, and shake my head. So this is the person I was warned about; the sophisticate who would play havoc with a simple soul like me, and stride off laughing. I look round for Scarlet Women. But there seem to be none in sight.

Lemady/Nurse Murdoch reaches round her desperately. She grabs a stone. "If we could sort of...I don't know. Pile rocks; anything...."

I shake my head again. Faith might well move mountains; what it can't do is pitch a big tent without pegs. "We'd better make a move; or it'll get late. It won't matter; where we are isn't important really. I'd like a beer though, first; not driving all that way without."

Lemady trails after me. For once, she hangs her head. I take no pleasure in it. Some would, no doubt; or at least rub salt. The sneering phrase "Wet" has yet to be coined; but I suppose that's what it makes me. I don't particularly care. It's a matter of priorities; and the priority is her. I'd like to turn the clock back, so her distress never happened; but that isn't possible.

There's no profit in such an attitude; not as profit is generally counted at least. I should use the knife, while I've got the chance; then when it was turned on me, I could weep. A *serein*; water from an empty sky. And the Nation of Shopkeepers would forgive me. But this isn't a subject for vivisection. It's Lemady.

We have reached the end of our stay. It was a magic time, despite, or maybe because of, the initial hiccup. We have to head back though; to *Tamesis Flumen*, yuppieland to be. The gear is packed; a final ceremony remains.

"I wouldn't mind a drink. Sort of a celebration. And to say cheerio to the place. For the moment anyway."

Lemady agrees. "Yes. I'd like that." Her eyes widen. "I can't go back to that pub though. I shall never go there again."

She made a mistake, before we left to retrieve the forgotten hardware. She knew it was wrong at the time; but she felt compelled. The landlord was sympathetic; it was the height of the season though, the few places in the village were full. He should know; he kept his finger firmly on the pulse of local affairs.

Silence fell as she spoke, in the little saloon bar. Eyes swivelled; on each face the same expression, in each mind the same thought. I suffered for her; but the crisis, I knew very well, was yet to come. This is it.

Just for once, I say the right thing. "Why not?"

I see the idea form, and take fire. "*Why not*," she says slowly. "*Why not indeed....*"

I watch her psych herself up. She takes a slow, deep breath, then another. Finally she straightens her shoulders, flicks her hair back.

"You fit?"

She nods. "Let's get on with it." She follows me across the road, toward the place of fear.

The same regulars are present, in the little room. The same silence falls. She observes them calmly, heads toward the bar. She perches on one of the high stools, crosses her legs. Her skirt is bright red, and short. For good measure, she hoists it another couple of inches. "I'll have a whisky, darling," she says languidly. "A large one, of course." If anything, the silence intensifies.

Mine host, like all good landlords, is a professional non-observer. He asks, politely, if we sorted out some accommodation. Lemady assures him we coped admirably. She asks if he has cigars. He produces a tin of slim black cheroots.

I've never seen her smoke; I didn't know she could. She takes a light, dribbles smoke from her nostrils in the approved fashion. Then she stares intently at each customer in turn. "Right," she's saying. "I'm the Whore of Babylon; and here I am. What are you going to do about me?" The talk rises again at once, becomes an anxious hubbub; each man seems suddenly preoccupied with what his neighbor has to say.

I thought I had begun to know her, just a little. I realize I hadn't started. She's The Rat from my Viking saga, turning on the Dancing Man who had so taunted her; she's Molly Zero; she's a whole lot else. And yet she's not. She is herself, nothing more; though certainly nothing less. Lines of force cross in her, as they cross at great Corfe Gate just down the road; there maybe is the link, between person and place.

My one-time employer buttonholes me. "How are you doing these days?" he asks casually.

"Oh, about the same. Getting by."

He flexes his knuckles, tenses the muscles of his neck and jaw. It's a favorite mannerism. It's presumably intended to convey authority; but a colleague once compared it to someone cracking nuts.

"I did rather well last week. Sold three story boards. I got more than you would have made for two books. Felt quite guilty actually."

"Congratulations."

He stares at me. "You told me you only got a hundred and fifty apiece for them."

"I told you when I started it was the standard rate for a first novel. They set a record last week; somebody got half a million."

His expression becomes beady. "So what did you get then? For your last thing?"

"Somewhere in between."

The same could be said of the relationship between fiction and what for want of a better term we call reality. The truth lies off at an angle; it's somewhere in between.

Though real events cast shadows. They're bound to; all things interrelate. "Tell me," says a man to whom I have been introduced, "do you really find life as complex and threatening as your books suggest?" The question is genuine; he has the English hardback of *Pavane* on his shelf, at first he hadn't connected the name.

"Yes."

He nods, thoughtfully. "Hmm. I was afraid you might...."

I listen to an interview with a well-known American pulp writer. The question of real life crops up. He seems genuinely surprised at the idea that it might relate to what he does. Leastways if he isn't, he's a damned good actor. Though I suppose he's been asked the same thing times enough before. He writes what he is asked for; what should that have to do with anything else?

33

It may be a sincere response of course. But if so, he has a curiously compartmented head. I would have thought such a division was impossible, attractive though the thought might be. The outmoded but intriguing notion of *Gestalt* has it that we change continuously, as experience and sensory input mount. So the Lemady who strode out of the pub wasn't the same woman who walked in; and I was not the same observer. How then can real events not influence our psyche? As they take place they enter it, become an integral part.

Employing details is a different matter. The memory bank is there to be drawn on. I use the tent peg episode; but as an aside, reduced to half a dozen words and in a different context. Later in *Gráinne*, the storyteller publishes a novel. To show her contempt for it, his mother rams it into the book case upside down. The same thing happened to me once; but using the episode doesn't indicate a vast hangup. I would never have thought of it for myself; the information seemed too bizarre to waste. We can't make up real life; as an artist can't make up the details of anatomy.

A writer and reviewer once formed a neat theory: that the stories I allowed to appear under pseudonym somehow contained an inner significance for me. I was amazed at her simplistic approach. The truth was that my editor of the time was convinced each piece in a collection must have a different byline, or the readers would feel cheated. So if anything it was the second-class stuff that was disguised. But she was undeterred. "Methinks he doth protest too much...." One could almost see the message passing across her forehead, like one of the electric signboards that were once such a vogue on newspaper buildings.

The comforting notion of the pigeonhole seems to be under increasing attack. More reason, I suppose, for its proponents to cling to it so firmly. At one time areas of the brain were neatly tagged, a duty assigned to each. Cases of hydrocephaly seem to have shown that at a need the cerebral cortex can take over the functions of the rest. The effect is not unlike that produced by Debussy's extraordinary tone poem, *La Mer*. Patterns shift and alter; the result is a sort of psychic dismay.

I read the autobiography of a well-known puppeteer. At one point he makes a suggestion. "When you have finished a figure, hold it and let it drop. Watch how it falls; it will have developed something of its own, regardless of what you tried to build in." Stories, and the characters in them, are much the same; they go their own way to an extent. The overall shape might be fixed; but the flavor of details changes. I suppose the same could be said for most enterprises; writing isn't magic or unique.

Gráinne is a case in point. Lemady would understand her; but she would only follow her a certain way. She is forceful where Lemady would withdraw. Finally, she courts death; but Lemady would not do that either. She loves life and its sensations, much as it might wound her. Like the sculptor of the Caliph's wondrous fountain.

So, a woman walks into a pub and braves the locals. A small event no doubt, inflated out of scale; but existence consists of small events. They string themselves together one after the next, like the pieces of the famous DNA spiral. And there are some who would sneer at anything. They measure their own stature, not mine. Or Lemady's.

Profit and loss; the concepts circle endlessly. Stare at them straight on and they lose meaning. They are mantras, like the famous Jewel in the Lotus; it's the underlying fallacy of western thought. In my novella, "Our Lady of Desperation," a painter and a civil servant square up to one another. It's a wonder I got the thing into print at all; certainly it was wildly and predictably misunderstood. One of the protagonists was an artist; so it was assumed I was somehow in his camp. In fact both are ratfinks; when thieves fall out, honest men, if they don't come into their dues, are at least afforded a wry smile.

Nonetheless, the painter makes a couple of fair points. "Escher *liked* crossword puzzles. Rubens *liked* large ladies. Picasso *liked* the color blue. It isn't a code; there's only what you see." It seems the notion is too simple to grasp; or too alarming. "I asked him why his shirtsleeves were rolled up," says a famous and intriguing movie actress, describing her first meeting with her future husband. "He said it was because he was hot." I find the answer equally riveting.

Logic isn't the commonest of traits; in the West at least. In my book *Kiteworld*, the Middler priest speaks of Godpath, main Cathedral of the Variants, the ruling order of the land. "A building is a concept. To decorate it with spires and pinnacles, to grace it with rich fabrics and many-colored glass; that is to make it gorgeous to the eye. But to say, 'This is a roof,' and 'These are walls. This is a doorway; these are windows, by which light may enter.' I sometimes wonder if that does not take more courage."

The vicar of Sts. Mary and Melor, parish church of Amesbury in Wiltshire, takes the point at once. I had thought he might be interested in the exploits of the proto-aviators; I have been told the history of flying is one of his enthusiasms. He agrees the hardware was well handled, but moves on rapidly. The tension between the adherents of the opposing faiths reminds him of certain aspects of his day to day parish work. He makes an admission; he found himself reading the book one day in his office. He wanted to know what happened to the Kitewaif, Velvet, when she put to sea in the storm. He felt guilty at first; then he changed his mind. "I thought perhaps this was work as well...." It makes me thoughtful in turn. It's one of the best compliments I was ever paid; but there's a great deal beyond that. In many ways Amesbury is the focus of my own sphere of magic. Here Elfrida came, after the murder of her stepson at Corfe Castle, to endow the first of her nunneries. A click, and the focus changes; here too came Guinevere, a misty, weeping Queen, fleeing the wrath of Arthur and his court. Much later I came this way myself, with Lemady. In those days you could drive straight on down the High Street, *en route* for Stonehenge a mile or so over the hill. I have the feeling a mystic circle has somehow been completed, or is nearing that state.

I am to read an intriguing book: *The Empty Mirror*, written by a young Westerner who spent a time in a Kyoto monastery. It's one of the elements that combine to produce *Gráinne*. At one point the acolyte describes how sitting on cold stone floors gives him a bad attack of piles. He complains to the Master of Novices that it seems a poor return for his attempted devotion.

When the remark is translated, his fellow monks lie down and kick their heels. They find the notion of cause and effect genuinely hilarious. Lemady may be the cause of a great deal; but the effects are nothing to do with her. The general takes over from the specific. To recreate the exact flavour of my time with her, to recreate other flavors; it's outside the scope of writing. A multi-track sense system would be required; and such a thing has yet to be devised. Despite the vaporings of the Virtual Reality buffs. In any case, to try would be to miss the point. The Russian film *Solaris* eschews for the most part the vulgarity of hardware. Instead, a profound question is posed. The simulacrum presented to the psychiatrist has the exact form of his wife; it must have, it was picked out of his brain. Is it therefore "real?" Is Lemady real, as she winds up the punters? If so, where does that leave the Whore of Babylon?

One must retrench, on what can seemingly be grasped. A friend turns up with a much-thumbed paperback. *Zen and the Art of Motorcycle Maintenance*, a book aimed very evidently at the Pulitzer Prize, that seemingly endless celebration of the values of small-town America. I am interested. Essentially, he is not what I think of as a reading man. An auto engineer, Rolls-Royce trained, a great deal besides, but literary; he has other fish to fry.

I ask him how he made out. He shakes his head a little mournfully. "Not too well, guv. Only got halfway. Felt I ought to have a go; but it wasn't for me."

"You did well. You got farther than I did."

He glances at me sharply. But we've known each other a long time; he knows I'm not sending him up. He turns the book. Predictably, the cover carries an image of a spanner gripping a lotus bud. He frowns. "That spanner's a Wilson Slim. They're no—beep—good at all. The steel's soft; use 'em a couple of times and they spread. Always keep one in the toolchest though; they're handy for non-standard nuts."

I congratulate him. I tell him he has just talked more Buddhism than I found in the book.

He looks pleased, but puzzled. "Is that a fact? Well, there's a thing. Wouldn't Adam and Eve it, would you?"

My friend is an unusual man in many ways. Women are attracted to him, it seems magnetically, as he is to them. He needs them, cannot be without; yet he genuinely has no time for them. Through him I meet a succession of intriguing girls; he has the habit of dumping them on me in a bar, having first made it plain that they are there for his later gratification. One of them is Maggie. I try to work out her background; but it's impossible. Her face is piquant, vivid; but the broad cheekbones, the short nose, the olive skin.... Eventually, I am forced to ask.

"Maggie, where do you hail from?"

She favors me with a smile. She names a village a mile or so away.

OK. I asked for that.

The grin gets broader. "You don't mean that though, do you? You mean my Ethnic Origins." She considers for a moment. "I'm not a nignog."

"I wouldn't mind in the slightest if you were. You know that. You'll have to tell me though. I just can't guess."

She relents. Her mother was Irish, her father Greek. But Kerry has already been born; boon companion to Kaeti, my magical East Ender. I've often wondered what Maggie would make of the book. I think she would like it.

I've wondered, too, what my Rolls-Royce mate would have made of Lemady. I know what he would have done; treated her with careful respect. But that would have been because she was a friend of mine. What his real opinion would have been, or hers of him; well, that's another matter. One that, almost certainly, would never have been revealed.

Consideration of the origins of characters leads to curious asides. At the odd Convention, and at other times, one question never failed to amuse. Or irritate, depending on my mood. "Do you write from your own experience?" The answer seems too obvious to make. I'm not a telepath; so how the hell can I write from anybody else's? But the question remains. It hints at a gap in awareness difficult or impossible to bridge. We are all locked inescapably into our own perceptions; if in doubt, try to visualize a color outside the visible spectrum. In the science fiction genre, the wildest alien is at heart an Earthman with a funny hat on. "Unimaginable," an adjective beloved by a certain type of exponent, is really a tautology. If something cannot be imagined, for us it can have no meaning.

I understand what's being hinted at of course, albeit in a woolly sort of way. Does what I write have any relation with real life? It's the same old question; but the answer is the same as well. In the field of drawing and painting, the term "abstract" is widely misunderstood. At least, it's widely misapplied. All artists abstract, in so far as they draw out, or try to draw out, the salient features of their subject; but truly non-representational painting has been rare. Nicholson perhaps, Yves Tanguy; Mondrian, about whom Dali made the classic comment, "Piet, nyet...." And of course, there's always Jack the Dripper. But even Ben Nicholson put jug handles on his "abstract" shapes, as a species of signature. The bottleneck of sensory perception is one none of us can avoid, whatever use we make of the results. I read once of a fan artist who started out drawing in the style of Michaelangelo, but gave it up because he found it too limiting. True ignorance is truly indomitable; visual illiteracy strikes again.

"Do you put real people into your books?" is another pearl of little worth. Speaking at Oxford once, I commented that the only way I could think of doing it was to make up a large folder, rush along behind them and shout, "Gotcher!" To my surprise, it drew a round of applause.

The answer seems to contradict the first. It doesn't though. Written characters are one thing, real folk something else. One may put you in mind of the other; but memory is the only link. One thing is virtually certain. The most careful pen portrait would not be recognized, even if attempted; our perceptions of ourselves are generally at wild variance with the perceptions of others. Burns had something to say about that of course. His famous couplet was allegedly written after watching a flea crawl across the bonnet of an expensively dressed woman. It puts me in mind of certain aspects of the Thames Valley. Other places too, of course. My late father once called me onto the fire escape that ran along outside his projection room. He leaned his elbows contentedly on the rail and stared down at the kitchen window of a dress shop opposite. The owner's wife, a very swep-up lady, had shaken a dog blanket onto the sill and was busily engaged cracking the resulting livestock. "And I must put on rubber gloves, and search the Peke for fleas...." As ever, Dylan Thomas has the situation in a nutshell. And him the most passionate and romantic of men. But eroticism and wild comedy always did go hand in hand. Like music; the slightest slip, at the most serious concert, and the audience is in fits. So the link must be more than usually profound.

There are exceptions to all general statements of course. I write a piece I call "The Grain Kings." An acquaintance takes exception to my portrayal of a barman working aboard a vast, futuristic combine harvester. I made my character Swiss; he's Swiss, so it follows the story is about him. Circumstantial of course; but proving it is going to be on the dodgy side. He is undeterred. "I hire smart little Jew-boy lawyer. East End. This time I get you...." It makes me wonder how many times he's tried before.

My colleague mentions the matter to a mutual friend; another legal eagle, this time of startling mien. But anybody who draws conclusions from the Mickey Mouse stickers on his briefcase, the spectacularly permed hair, just hasn't looked carefully into his eyes. He asks what I have called my character.

"Swissy..."

"Bloody fool. I'll take it...."

A libel threat has been made; so I'm duty bound to report it. I finish up in a sacred purlieu indeed; Lincoln's Inn, no less. Halfway through the meeting a disturbed gentleman chuffs into the office. The firm's senior partner has collapsed in his bathroom; they're trying to break the door down to reach him. Nothing like this has happened since seventeen sixty. My colleague, who has come along for the experience, is duly impressed. So am I. It's something for me to be able to produce a new aspect of London; he's produced enough for me.

Nothing comes of the threatened legal action. I hardly expected it would; though that didn't make the experience any more pleasant. My assailant obviously thought all he had to do was blow a whistle, and I would give him a million pounds. But there's a little more involved than that. A famous jurist once coined a memorable remark. "The law is like the Savoy hotel. Anyone can use it."

If one admits to being influenced by real events, or accepts the inevitability, the charge of autobiographic writing usually rears its head. Leastways, I think it's a charge; I always found it puzzling. Autobiography is one thing, fiction another; though certain politicians may have blurred the edges a little. Such a hybrid notion would surely be hard to handle. Having to stick to real events, in a fixed order, would play havoc with the story line. While planning *The Boat of Fate*, a novel set at the end of the Roman occupation of Britain, I feared just such inhibiting factors. I was cured quite early on by a Professor of Archaeology who was generous enough to give me a seminar. "Well," he said, after recharging my sherry glass, "you'd better ask the questions; and I'll see if I can answer them."

That seemed eminently reasonable; so I plunged in at the deep end. "Sir," I said, "when did the Roman occupation of Britain actually end?"

He considered. "That depends on two things. One, what you mean by the Roman occupation of Britain; and two, what you mean by it ending." Some months later, after I had worked through the extensive reading list he had supplied, I began to see what a stupid question I had asked; and how profound his answer had been.

"You mean they don't know either? I thought it was all cut and dried...."

Yes. I thought they blew a whistle too, and all dashed off to take part in the Decline and Fall.

"Planning" is equally a misnomer for the construction of the book. I've traveled with Lemady to see a Roman villa I've read a lot about. I fall in love with the place on sight; the cluster of half-timbered buildings, set at the head of a shallow valley. There's an air of serenity; but there seems to be something more. Between the wicket gate and the pay desk, the outline of a story comes to me. In physical terms, I suppose the distance is about thirty yards. I turn to Lemady. "I'm going to write a book about Roman Britain."

She eyes me carefully. "That's nice," she says.

The ensuing year is spent not so much on background research as confirmation of what I had already scribbled down. Some of the verifications are striking. At one point in the story the main character had invited the villain of the piece, a disaffected slave, to eat with him. His intention was to show goodwill prior to setting him free. I find in the late fourth century, to share a table before witnesses was an accepted ritual of manumission.

Some aspects are more problematic of course. I put one to the Professor.

"You see my difficulty, sir. Either they built another bath house right beside the first, which means they were pretty well off; or it was a fulling shed. They'd had to turn the place into a clothing factory. I'm sure they wouldn't have done that. Not if they were really landed gentry...."

He makes a curious snuffling sound, like the dog in the famous cartoon series. I realize he's laughing. You pays your money, he seems to be saying, and you takes your choice. So much for the Groves of Academe.

Some years later I go back to the Villa. A lot has changed. A continuous video display fills in the background for visitors, and the collection in the little site museum has been enhanced by recent finds. One in particular takes my eye; a roughly-cast bronze buckle, shaped like a dolphin with its tail in its mouth. "From the harness of a soldier of the late fourth century," announces the new, glossy guidebook. "Who he was, and what he was doing at Chedworth, will never be known." It fits in beautifully though. My protagonist dropped it when he stormed out, after the master of the place laid on a sex show for the benefit of the barbarian from Rome.

I show the guide to my colleague. It makes him thoughtful.

"It's quite understandable. A fourth century man told me his story. I called him Sergius. It only took a few seconds. I just had to write it down."

In itself, the coincidence is not surprising. There would have been soldiers everywhere in that confused, distant time, the remnants of what had once been the garrison of Britannia. One might easily have tried to organize a doomed defense of the place I called Censorina. There's just one snag. The Villa wasn't gutted in a wild attack, though doubtless there were many that were. It was deserted, and fell into gentle decay; hence, presumably, the gentle vibes. As ever, the "truth" of fiction stands at an angle from the "truth" of fact. That way, Elfrida and Guinevere can coexist.

Such an episode might tempt some into Spiritualist maunderings; but there's really no need for them. The thought process itself is mysterious and fascinating enough. To start with, it's instantaneous; as far as our perceptions are concerned at least. One moment an idea isn't there, the next it is. It may be added to, developed; but there's no conscious period of formation.

I'm chatting to a young man I've not seen for a couple of months. He has his daughter with him; a pretty little girl, just past the toddler stage. She points to the bar, the display of cordial bottles. "May I have some orange juice please?" I am arrested. Previously, she would indicate her choice clearly enough; "orange," "lemon," or whatever had taken her eye. But a sea-change has been wrought. There must have come a moment when she realized words could be strung together to make their own superior sense, when the concept of the sentence dawned. And life irrevocably changed. The new notion of evolution makes more sense at once; a series of explosive developments, triggered by environment, rather than a process of steady, undetectable change. After all, what would be the need for it? Cockroaches have been around for years enough; and they haven't altered much. They are a successful organism; they have found their niche. So there would be no point.

The question of Sergius can never be resolved of course. Maybe some essence did "come through," for that brief moment; perhaps Lemady summoned it, unknowing. The trick is to establish the contrary; as ever, one is faced with the burden of negative proof. It's another of the Unanswerable Questions, on which the Gotama firmly turned his back. There's something comforting in the process. If only we could achieve it more often, at least we would lead calmer lives. "Ere nescience shall be reaffirmed, how long, O Lord, how long?"

Hardy at his most profound. For he could be profound on occasions. Get the carping over first by all means; what's left is the nitty-gritty.

I'm hailed, or assailed, by an old friend. He looks like a Chief Engineer, he talks like one; and by God, that's exactly what he was.

He engages me on the subject of literature. In his view, Burns was the finest poet ever to write in English.

"OK, Wattie. You keep Burns, we'll keep Shakespeare."

He walks away and drums his fingers. I notice the back of his neck has gone dark red, and is bulging. Finally he comes back. "Laddie," he says with a sort of quiet intensity, "I'll tell you something. You're the only person to have insulted Burns on my birthday, and *lived*...."

Right. Let's get down to cases. And not so much, truly, in self defense. Who can read "Bonnie Doon" without at least a stinging of the eyes? "Ye'll break my heart, ye warbling bird, that warbles on the flowing thorn. Thou minds me o' departed joys, departed never to return...." We end up crying on each other's shoulders; and Wattie reads extracts of *M'Andrew's Hymn* for me, pausing from time to time to explain technicalities I hadn't fully understood. "How could he know so much?" he asks wonderingly, staring at the *Collected Kipling* with its old, embossed swastika. I realize I'm extremely fortunate; and not just for being still alive.

Though care is always needed when dealing, or attempting to deal, with Wattie. He bristles with sensitivities; I've come across such things since. At first he much approved of Lemady; the very sight of her seemed to act as a moustache-conditioner. Then I let slip, inadvertently, that she was Scottish; a Scot without an accent. Instantly, the Highland/Lowland antipathy rears its head; she becomes "yon bliddy lassie." She smiles a little sadly when I tell her. "I can understand that. He's a Glaswegian; they don't like people like me. It's all rather silly...." It's how folk are though, for the most part. Even on occasions expansive, outgoing folk like Wattie. Bigotry, class consciousness; they're like what I've heard called egoboo, they get in the way of what really matters. Sometimes nations fall as a result; sometimes it's merely enterprises. Like publishing good books. Either way, it's tragic; or seems to be at the time. But all States are subject to Change.

IV.

On occasions, Time, the uncontrollable dimension, seems to become a little less opaque. It "wears thin," to quote a metaphor that itself has got a little ragged at the edges. Maybe that's what happens though.

I'm walking the perimeter of Avebury, the greatest stone circle of them all. I did that once with Lemady; but she is no longer present, except maybe as a shade. Instead, Tammy is with me. She modeled for me once, to my faint surprise. My colleague Peter Pearce took the shots. He made her laugh, fooling with a quadruple-extension tripod; an hour later we were sitting at ease in a pub of our choice. "This," he observed, handing drinks round, "is the part of a photography session I like best...."

Examining the contacts, I asked him why he had moved so fast. He answered instantly. "She was nervous, she was tensing up. It had to be quick; she'd have got worse, not better." I hadn't noticed; I was too intent on the results. But portrait photography starts like a lot of other things, between the ears. Pressing the button is the last stage in the process, not the first.

The erstwhile model looks round her thoughtfully; at the megaliths, the great circling ditch. Something seems to be preoccupying her. Finally she turns. "How did they shave? In those days?"

"Well, it was difficult. You can't get much of an edge on a bronze razor. Least, I wouldn't think so. So most of them didn't bother."

She tosses her mop of auburn curls. "Uggh. I can't *stand* men with beards...."

I can't explain why I laugh so much. She exists at a point, as Lemady existed at a point, blazing into her pub; and the world, all fantasies, rotate about her. Five thousand years or so make little difference. The odd change of fashion perhaps; but her essential femaleness remains. It's the true expression of her timelessness. Kaeti, my little East End sprite, is the same; but the trade, such as it is, recoils with horror. Fantasy, like all genres, has its own rigidly-applied rules; you can't be in touch with Eternal Truths if you drop your aitches.

Actually I wouldn't lay odds on the effectiveness or otherwise of a Bronze Age razor; or any other ancient tool, come to that. A Professor of Archaeology I met once by chance taught me caution in that respect. Leastways, he must have been a Professor; certainly the young man he was lunching with, on bread and cheese in my local, treated him with a deference that obviously came of long practice. The Prof. asked a question about his colleague's current state of funding, and was surprised by the answer. "Five thousand?" he said incredulously. "Five *thousand*, for a *Palaeolithic*?" The Enterprise Culture was still in full blast; fortunes were to be made, or so it seemed, merely by shooting one's mouth off and being malicious to the disadvantaged. But real culture was already feeling the draught.

Later, the subject of hand axes crops up. The uses to which they were put is apparently still a subject for learned debate, in some circles at least. "I was wondering," says the disciple mildly, "if the worked edge was meant for insertion into a stick or stave. Then you bashed people with the other bit."

He smiles, brightly; his elder and better regards him with a certain expression, and he retreats into his beer. "The hand axe," proclaims the Prof., "is a product of the imagination...." Which would seem to settle things; except that he immediately embarks on an account of an experiment recently conducted at his local butcher's shop. A single stroke with one of the great flints apparently almost cut a side of bacon in half, to the moderate annoyance of the proprietor. Looking at the breadth of the experimenter's shoulders, and the size of his hands, I can quite believe it. Maybe my own mentor was right; the days of Academe are numbered, if they're not completely over. Pity the literary world hasn't caught up. Then, Desdemona might be allowed to drop her aitches, and Helen of Troy as well. Wonder of wonders, they might even be permitted the odd glottal stop. True, an account of a Stone Age tryst I saw recently read like a happening at a kinky Tupperware party; but that was merely brainless writing. Do it deliberately and you'd be in the worst sort of trouble; your breathless public would suspect you were sending them up.

I am to construct a mock-Mediaeval legend round the strange name of a New Forest glade. Apparently it sits happily enough with the collection for which it was intended, and it's later snapped up for reprint by an American mag. It's cast in the formal, rather stilted language expected of such things. If I really wanted to sell regardless, and go on selling, I would imitate it more often. "Great Ghu, do you mean the ring of Howsyourfather has failed? Then sound the Horn of Oojahkaflip; but remember, it can only be sounded once...." You crank the handle, and out it pours; endlessly, or so it seems. Fine if that's what you want; markets are there to be supplied. And as I've always carefully pointed out, the loss is mine; in more ways than one. But I get bored. Tàm/Lemady, clattering the hangers in the Gift Shop and falling in love with everything in sight, seems much more vital. Most folk who try to be themselves experience similar problems; unless of course the "self" clicks in with current vogues. It's like dragging a ton weight up an endless slope. Sooner or later you have to take a rest; and then as like as not the thing will trundle back to the start. Like the ambulance in the famous film.

The remarkable early photographer Frank Meadow Sutcliffe, recorder of the extraordinary world of Victorian Whitby, once took a portfolio of photographs to London. The dealer he approached flicked through them disdainfully. At that time sitters were posed in studios, in front of large painted backdrops; I've seen such things for myself, still *in situ*. These studies were realistic; they looked nearly like paintings themselves. That wasn't the way to go about things at all. Meadow Sutcliffe confided to his diary that it was the first time he had realized one could fail by doing a thing too well. He was still young; but the iron had already entered his soul.

Staying with me in Wiltshire, Tam makes an admission. "You know when you and Peter picked me up to do that cover shot? My mother was dead worried. She said not to let you talk me into taking my clothes off. I didn't tell you before; I thought you'd be annoyed."

"That was silly of her. It was the clothes we wanted really. We were after a sort of Thirties look."

"Thanks a lot," she says sharply. But she knows I don't mean it. Not completely anyway. She has already had a go at my colleague, along lines not wholly dissimilar.

"It must have been very boring for you, taking pictures of me. I'm not much to look at."

"Oh, I wouldn't say that," he observes mildly. "I spent yesterday photographing slurry pumps. You really are much prettier...." You don't catch old birds with chaff; he hasn't brought up a family of his own for nothing.

Nonetheless, the comment makes me thoughtful. When I was very young, one of the images I had of myself in later life was of a dirty old man in a mac. Why, I'm not certain; an inbuilt tendency to moroseness perhaps. Later, there were many more interesting things to do than look at dirty books. Maybe though some people never get beyong that stage.

While praising the novel Tam illustrated for us, a reviewer expresses disappointment at the packaging. "A pity it's merely a photograph...." That was to be expected though. Artwork is in vogue at the moment. It's bound to be better than a "mere photograph." Even bad artwork. After all, it's done by hand. And anyway, the thing has already served its purpose.

There are two sorts of people in the advertising world; and outside it, come to that. Those who understand their job, and those—

much in the majority—who pick up buzz words, make a lot of noise round the edges. They raise a constant background chatter, like Kipling's Bandar-Log. After a while, one finds one can mostly tune it out.

I've been taken, by a client, to the Royal Overseas League in St. James. It's an amazing establishment; where else for instance would one come across an elderly, military-looking gentleman snoring blissfully beneath a potted palm, an empty gin bottle at his side? I am introduced, maliciously, to a well-known author. From the way the thing is done, my companion is obviously expecting fireworks. They don't materialize. My new acquaintance knows *Pavane*, the book that has become something of a millstone round my neck; as *Lorna Doone* became a millstone for R. D. Blackmore. The reason isn't far to seek. Faced with the chore of writing blurbs, editors copy each other; it's easier than thinking. So once someone picks up on a book its title is perpetuated from wrapper to wrapper. We rapidly get onto the subject. My friend was an Agency copywriter once on a time; we talk the same language. The client, disappointed, wanders off, starts to pump money into a fruit machine.

Effectively, we come from different worlds; my colleague was top of the best-seller lists for a time before being pushed from his perch by, as he puts it, "B-bloody Solzhenitsyn." Advertising is the link; and many of our beefs are curiously the same. Editors know little of promotion; they have a piece of paper that declares them literate—a Degree, it's called—but that's about all. For years now I've been leaving a desk littered with copy and artwork, only to be told that "authors don't know about that sort of thing." For a while, I thought it might induce a personality crisis.

We trade information at high speed for an hour. After which my friend prepares to leave. He has to meet his wife; they're tax exiles, they come to London twice a year on shopping sprees. Before he goes though, I feel I have to ask him at least one interviewer-type question. He tells me to go ahead. I leaf through a mental list.

"Do you identify with the heroes of your stories?" He draws himself up. "What do you think?"

"I asked you."

He glares at me. "N-none of the buggers stammer, do they?" Then he is gone, into what I suppose one might call the Great Swirl of the City.

Memories of that particular time abound. Many episodes took place in surroundings that were spectacular, or to say the least historic. Years before, my colleague had thoughtfully made himself a life member of the reconstituted Wig and Pen Club, housed in an ancient building in the Strand that was one of the few in that part of the city to survive the Great Fire. It became a favorite port of call; to sit and sip ale, stare across to the Law Courts and wait for the papers to come round and the tray of cheese on toast, was an experience unlike any other, though had my proclivities been more generally known the fannish description of myself as a middle class Prospero would have been succeeded by something even more dire or daft. Incidents there were in plenty; my favorite is the time when Peter, who was facing the door, asked mildly if I would believe him if he said an African chief in full regalia had just walked into the room.

The surroundings seemed to call for Johnsonian responses. "Of course I would; but damn it man, you don't expect me to turn round and *look* at him, do you?" At least it amused the gentleman at the next table; he all but choked on his beer. Though my small offering was rapidly surpassed. The Chief in question, a huge and impressive man in beautiful white and yellow robes, was rapidly surrounded by a crowd of hooray Henrys, all vying with each other to engage him in conversation. One pointed at a massive stick he was carrying, carved from what seemed to be ebony. "I say, Chief, is that your staff of office?" The object of attention turned it and smiled. "No," he said in a soft *basso profondo*. "Bought it in Bond Street this morning. Silly bloody thing, isn't it?" You can't beat lines like that; the moral is, don't even try.

The Prospero crack, as I recall, was made shortly after the appearance of my short story collection, *Ladies from Hell*. The theme that linked the various pieces was that of the individual *versus* State oppression, of whatever hue. In the opening story, "Our Lady of Desperation," I posited among other things that England had fallen under the control of a Civil Service mandarin; nonetheless, disappointment was expressed because all my threats came "from the Left." Maybe I'm politically colorblind; but I can't imagine a more right-wing villain myself.

Actually I've got a good idea what started the frothing; a throwaway line in another of the stories that took a not very worthy swipe at a couple of prominent Socialists who had temporarily annoyed me. It was the sort of thing I would normally edit out; but my attention momentarily lapsed, and it slipped through. Pity. There's an old saying about not being able to win 'em all; but it doesn't make unguarded moments any less irritating.

"Our Lady" continued to create confusion in a variety of quarters. Another idea that had come along was the notion of what I called negatax. In the society I devised, liberal ideas had progressed to the point where tax fines had completely replaced custodial sentences. So when individual loadings exceeded a hundred per cent, the State paid the difference to keep miscreants solvent. A reviewer for a magazine I had previously respected wasted half a page of ink attacking what she termed my shaky economic theories. I was considerably surprised. It

seemed she had not come across what I would have considered a fairly
widespread writing ploy; it's called satire. Not that I felt like com-
plaining. To buy that much advertising space would have cost a bomb;
I, or rather the publishers, had got it for free.

The story had what I suppose one might call its world *première*
at Oxford; leastways I based a talk round it, some months before publi-
cation. Again I had the feeling a critical event was somehow taking
place; certainly an unrepeatable one. One of the extracts I had selected
for reading concerned the negatax system, and how it came about. As I
detailed the protagonist's case, chuckles began to break out; the audience was that far ahead of the punchline. When it finally came, it had a
quality of bathos they found hilarious. Unwittingly, I had tapped the
same vein tapped by Gerard Hoffnung in his classic tale of the accident-
prone builder. As his unfortunate trustingly fills the oil drum with
bricks, the audience at the Oxford Union begins to gurgle with anticipation. By the time he unties the rope they are holding their sides. He
announces the thing was heavier than he was, and hysteria breaks out;
at which he delivers the ultimate in anticlimactic comments. "*And I began to ascend....*" A whole succession of laughs for the price of one; it
could barely have happened anywhere else.

I was asked later on why I had not taped my session. I hadn't
thought to; it's a pity though. At least it would have proved I once had
the same effect on an audience as one of the greatest modern humorists.

The talk began at nine; it was scheduled to end at ten thirty. I
did it without a watch. Not bravado, but necessity; mine had elected to
turn its electronic toes up the night before. I paced the thing as well as
I was able, hoping I was getting it about right. I reached the end finally, and closed the folder. "Thank you, ladies and gentlemen. That's
your lot...." As I laid the thing down, the College clock began to
chime the half hour. Well, I'd never do that again; I decided there and
then it was best not to try.

Chatting to a group of students afterward, I outlined some of
the attacks I already knew would be made. "You had no trouble with it
though. Seemed to quite like it...." The young man I was addressing
looked thoughtful, then slightly pained. "What does one say? After
all, this *is* Oxford...."

He was right of course, unpalatable though the remark might
be in certain quarters. If the thing had failed before those vivid folk,
I'd have judged it stood no chance anywhere. I can almost hear the cry
of elitism going up though. "But there must be excellence," said Lady
Antonia Fraser once, in the midst of a heated education debate. "There
must be excellence...." I agree with her. If that makes me some sort of
screaming right-winger, then so be it. But I don't think it does. Neither would Lemady.

I am sent the text of a soon-to-be-published novel. A photocopy, naturally; the craze for Bound Uncorrecteds has just started, they're worth good money now. Despite, or maybe because of, the NOT FOR RESALE notice blazoned across the front of each. The editor concerned asks me if I can "write some quotes" that would be suitable for the wrapper. It's an extraordinary request; nearly as extraordinary as Hammer Films, who at one point took to dreaming up lists of titles and circularizing agents to ask if they had any books that matched. One cannot really "write quotes," it's a sort of contradiction in terms. I say I'll do a short review, and he can extract anything that takes his fancy. The finished job is actually a piece of promotion copy in itself. I'm careful to avoid any qualifications. Publishers have an unerring nose for the anti-sell; and whatever label is attached will stay with the book for life.

I'm right. It does. Even when the paperback house rises to the giddy heights of six inch doubles in the London dailies. I'm glad I made my effort bombproof.

Many years ago I wrote a book in the style of the late, much admired John Wyndham. Science fiction was popular at the time, the "English disaster novel" an accepted sub-genre. I'm not suggesting comparisons; nonetheless, they were made. I was loudly condemned as a "pastiche" writer; strictly a misnomer, to pastiche is to filch indiscriminately from here and there. *The Furies* was a deliberate homage to one man. One of the most vociferous accusers later became skilled in the art of real pastiche himself; but I suppose that was only to be expected, once the idea had entered his mind.

I didn't write what for want of a better term is called science fiction again; or at least, not very often. It was too late though; I had not allowed sufficiently for the pigeonhole mentality. The label had been attached; and it's well known, in England at least, that science fiction writers are semi-literate at best. "We've often featured non-intellectual subjects," writes the BBC producer of the annual program *Mastermind*, in answer to an hilarious charge of elitism. "Like sport, and science fiction...." Most writers who have received the tag have similar problems, though of course they don't admit it. Instead they winge to their nearest and dearest, on the fond assumption that it won't get out; the rest is egoboo.

As might be expected, Doris Lessing puts things much more into perspective. Explaining her own forays into the field she observes, not with irritation but with the air of someone who has been called on to spell out the obvious far too often before, that the "social novel" is a purely modern invention, barely four hundred years old. Before, all was Wonder Tale, from the time of Homer onwards. Logically, the strands should coexist; after all, Charlotte Brontë was born the year before Jane Austen died. But it is not permitted. Lessing is a distinguished writer; *i.e.*, she has made a few bob for her publishers, almost certainly despite their ministrations. So the aberration may be forgiven. Authors do that sort of thing from time to time; she'll soon get back on the rails.

The same remark was made about me when I wrote my second book, *Pavane*. The American editors of the time were particularly indignant. Now if a space ship had zoomed down, to sort out the Cavaliers and Roundheads; that would have been something they could identify with. Relate to. Amusingly, the English fans took quite the opposite tack. The thing was dazzlingly original; in some mysterious way it had sprung ready-armed from nowhere. The war that broke out between the Norman and Angevin factions after the Conquest, the fine work of the historical novelist Alfred Duggan, had obviously not figured in their course of studies. I had even built the title of one of his books into the text; but the point was not picked up.

Except once. A young acquaintance edges up to me, I think in the old "Load of Hay" in Paddington. He smiles broadly, murmurs "Leopards and Lilies" and slips away again. But he's the only one. It's an illustration of the narrowness of interest of a lot of folk; or another example of the pigeonhole principle. It's far from unique to publishers; they can't even claim originality for that.

I discover at an early stage the sort of ghetto into which I am in danger of being thrust. An Important Author—so important even he has had to acknowledge the fact—wants a new masthead for a mag he is theoretically to edit. "I saw a typeface called *Grot*," he screams, sweating with excitement. "That's what I want. *Grot*...."

I explain as patiently as I am able that letter designs fall into two sorts. If they have little points on their feet, they are serif faces; if not, they are Grotesques. If he can discover which of the innumerable possibilities has caught his eye, I will obtain it for him. Until such time, there is nothing to be done.

He is not soothed. On the contrary, the stridulation becomes worse. Any moment, he will surely begin to froth at the mouth. "Get this fool out of here," he shrieks. "I want *Grot*...*Grot*...."

He needn't worry, I'm already on my way. Mr. Wackford Squeers, the proprietor of Dotheboys Hall, had but one eye; Dickens points out, with vivid wit, that popular prejudice runs in favor of two. My prejudice is for sanity; the company of copywriters and the like.

Tammy has proceeded to the trying-on of hats. Not far off, the greatest of the sarsens nuzzles into a little lane. "Like a horse come for sugar" I wrote once, trying, vainly perhaps, to express the layered strangeness of the place. I knew the work of Paul Nash, the English landscape painter, long before I took up the formal study of art; "Landscape of the Megaliths," "Equivalents for the Megaliths," and all the rest. In one way, my book *The Chalk Giants* was a celebration of him. But again, one has to be careful. *"Art?"* shrieks an enraged fan. *"Art..?"* The inverted snobbery of the truly confused surges instantly to the fore. I wonder what the word, admittedly unsatisfactory, conveys to such folk. Somebody swanning about perhaps, hand to forehead, being "creative" and looking down on the herd. I have news they will maybe find surprising. It isn't us that do that; it's them. During World War Two, the lithographer Barnett Friedman was commissioned to produce a painting of the control room of a submarine. He refused to start the job till he had learned the function of every valve and control; he felt he owed it to the men who risked their lives there. "Art" is an attitude of mind. It's also universal; Tammy, trying her silly hats on, is high art indeed.

My landlady in Waitrose-on-Thames gets herself a job at a little local hospital, repairing the torn clothes of disturbed children. Also the torn clothes of the doctors' families; at least, till she puts her foot down. A week or so passes; then she asks a question. "What's the actual meaning of the word asylum?"

I tell her it was originally a place of refuge. Folk still ask for asylum in the political sense.

She nods. "Then that place is an asylum two times over. For the patients, and for the staff."

I feel I have learned a considerable truth. An asylum, or a ghetto, can shoot back. It's uncomfortable though, to be caught in the crossfire.

Lemady seems endlessly to recreate herself. She has that knack as well. She is here, she is gone; she disappears, and she is there again. My artist of "Our Lady of Desperation" has the final word, unpleasant opportunist though he is. He never married his Nymph; he preferred to keep on finding her afresh.

"Why do you always end up with the prettiest girls?" asks a customer at my local pub aggrievedly. "What's the secret?" The owner of the hotel down the road is more blunt. He advances forcefully, leans burly forearms on the bar. He glances at my companion. "Tell me something, Keith. Isn't it about time you stood aside, gave us youngsters a chance? We always have to make do with second-raters."

I consider. It's only the Clocktower Girl, or the shell of what she used to be. If he only knew, he could have her with a quarter of tea. But he doesn't know; he isn't a thinking man.

"Well, I'll tell you how it is, Brian. I'm not as active as I was, I can't run as fast. So I have to let them come to me, and leave the rest to you."

The smile remains; but his eyes become pure flint. So that's another place where I shall have to watch my back. Doing no harm carries dangers of its own. In an ideal world, it would be a passport; but this is Waitrose-on-Thames.

The secret, if it can be so dignified, seems obvious enough. Lemady, or whatever name she currently adopts, knows she's safe. Her occasional confessions are safe as well. "You've got to realize," says an acquaintance nasally, "you're just a father-figure to these girls." Again, the answer seems too obvious to make. If they told their fathers the half of what they come out with to me, they would brain them. I stand in no relationship, except perhaps that of trust. So I can't have been too bad a bloke overall, despite what's often been said.

It seems increasingly, Lemady is a complex package. She's like the yet-to-be-marketed Walkman; compact, but filled with extraordinary things. She can replicate herself of course; while the working of her mind is equally involved, even her so-called climaxes a subject for debate. She keeps it that way, deliberately; for she is nothing if not an accomplished actress. Intimacy, in one sense, brings her no closer; but such things are too obvious to dwell on. She is perennially fascinating; but that is because she is fascinated by herself. And with her own kind; there is an equally endless turning inward. Lemady observes a young waitress. "She's got a good figure. And she's a really nice girl, I can tell. Why don't you go with her? She'd do you much more good than me." There is an intensity in her awareness; something far removed from the innuendos of the gutter press. And equally far from earth-tides, and all the rest. These days, I leave those for the fantasists. Come to think of it, I always did. Or tried to.

Awareness comes by steady stages of course; it cannot be forced. At least, it's most ill-advised to try. The reverse is equally true. A secretary-bird I have known for some time, a bright, attractive girl—not to say downright sexy—reflects ruefully on her own Convent schooling. "The Sisters used to tell us to look straight ahead when we were bathing, never at our bodies. It made us start wondering of course. Least, it did me. 'What's this bit for then? I wonder what that does....'" The principle involved is the same one that's invoked by telling children not to run on the grass; it's the surest way to little trails of heel-prints. I believe the general term for it is Induction.

If Lemady's responses are diffuse, those of the average male, it seems, are tediously direct. I'm sitting in a pub in Waitrose-on-Thames. I'm observing a group of young people in the far part of the bar. One of the girls is black, and her face is very striking. Her high cheekbones, long-tailed eyes, make her look like an Easter Island statue; or the decorative masks certain of the South Sea Islanders carved on the prows of their canoes. Also, she radiates evil; a rare quality, but not to be mistaken. Some sort of trouble seems to be brewing between two of the youths; and she is fanning the flames. Her eyes gleam; she wants to see blood, and is not particularly bothered who it belongs to. I have already gauged the distance to the door. The first sound of breaking glass and I'm away. I came out for a quiet drink, not to scrape up pieces of other people.

The landlord nudges me. "She pretty, dat one; eh, Keit'?" (He is not English). "Yes," I say absently. "Unusual face."

He looks concerned; for him, a rare expression. "Eh, Keit'. You not touch her, eh? She trouble, dat one. I tell you...."

"Of course I'm not going to touch her. I just said she had an interesting face."

"No," he says. "You watch it wit' dat one, I tell you. You leave her alone...."

"For God's sake, Ed. Give it a rest...."

But it seems the needle has stuck. I begin to understand. He only has one thought in mind; and with him, observation equals action. He is incapable of conceiving otherwise.

The trouble subsides; much, I'm sure, to the unknown girl's disappointment. But I leave anyway, to be free of his nagging.

I speak to my colleague on the phone. I mention a Government Minister I just saw on TV. Mostly, public figures wear a good face when they can; he is unable to disguise his arrogance and choler, even for the cameras. Peter chuckles. "If you met him in a pub in the Thames Valley...."

"If he was running it I'd be banned anyway. If he was a customer I'd have to watch myself; he'd be bound to have his mates with him." While if I walked in with a woman, Lemady or any other.... If it's got a skirt on and it's within sight, that type consider it their property. Maybe it's a necessary fact of life; evolution, Dominant Males and all the rest. I've even heard the principle invoked as an excuse; but the reality is a pain. We're really a pretty undeveloped species.

The A4 is not always so inviting. Lemady has decreed we go to Bath. I set out. It rains. Better than that, it pelts down. I grind through Chippenham and all points west, peering through a bleary windscreen at the tailboards of lorries. My temper worsens steadily.

We're late arriving. Almost at the end of lunch. And the city isn't what it was to become. Then, briefly, the hallways of houses were priced at 20K. The first place we try has no menu. The second is nearly as bad. They can do bangers and mash; the rest is "orf."

A devil is in Lemady. "But I *like* bangers and mash. I always have. Ever since I was at school...."

I leave in search of a loo. When I get back, she is surrounded by what in former times would have been called Traveling Men. They scatter at my approach. But I suppose a large, bad-tempered person bearing down can look a little daunting; even if it's only me.

The potatoes when they arrive are blueish and unappetizing. I fiddle with a fork. "If you tell me you like lumpy spuds as well, I'll crown you...."

I give the meal up as a bad job and push the plate away. "How this place ever became famous for buns defeats me...."

"Thank you, sir," says the manageress icily.

The Baths are disappointing. But by that time I'm no longer in a mood to be pleased by anything. An attendant shows off some recent excavations. He touches a switch; a bank of floodlights explodes with a loud crack. "*Ho*" he says. He really does have one of those sort of voices. He tries again. The same result. Undeterred, he continues from subterranean gloom. "Well, this all became famous two thousand years ago. And that, as you will realize, is a *very long time*...."

"Christ," I say. I leave.

The Abbey proves the last straw. Despite the marvelous Jacob's ladders.

I take one look inside and turn on my heel. "A vertical cemetery...."

I flee to Wells. On the road, the sun comes out. Glastonbury Tor shows, tiny with distance. It's the saving of the day.

There are roughnesses and setbacks from time to time. I suppose there are with all relationships. For the most part, I'm ignoring them as insignificant. It's not a case of rosy glasses; I've worn specs since I was a small boy, but they've always remained obstinately untinted. In any case, if I'm to pour ashes on my head it will be in private. I always distrusted public exhibitions of guilt; I've heard them described as penances with hooks.

Time passes. We are on the Hampshire/Dorset border. Lemady has found a little church, set on its own in fields. Round it, magically, is the embankment of an ancient British fort. So the church was placed deliberately, to consecrate the site. A Little Owl watches us calmly, perched atop a sign from the Ministry of Works.

Once more, lines of force seem to cross. She couldn't have called the owl; to that exact place, at that exact time. Or could she? Anything seems possible; or more precisely perhaps, nothing seems impossible.

My eyes have begun to stream. There is a pig unit opposite. Lemady seems not to notice. "Oh, that," she says, when her attention is finally drawn. "It's only a country smell. I got used to them years ago...."

The plane she is inhabiting doesn't seem for the moment to include the existence of manure. I wish I could say the same for mine.

The evening is warm; and I'm thirsty. "I saw a pub just down the road. Doesn't look much outside, but at least we could get a drink. Shandy, anything; I don't really mind."

"Yes," she says with equal vagueness. "That would be nice...."

As we leave, the owl flies away. I am faintly irritated by the collision of symbols. Like Ashenden being annoyed by the beauty of the Swiss lakes. The symbols existed though, and came together; as the lakes exist. To deny them would be to deny a section of reality. The determined hopelessness of the kitchen sink school is as unacceptable as the steely hygiene of romantic fiction. The thing to do is to find a middle way. It's just that it's hard, with Lemady.

V.

I have to pick a cheque up from my ex-employer. Leastways, I don't have to; but it makes life easier. It feeds his ego if I fetch them; while I can get my money without too much waiting about.

Lemady has said she'll drive me up; it isn't all that far. She has heard of him vaguely; she's curious to see his pad. We wait in the car for the great man to appear.

He got back in touch because of the first Spitfire I acquired. Buying it was nothing to do with a macho image; at that time they were the cheapest cars on the list, and I was tired of dusting back seats I never used. In any case I liked the Michelotti styling. But owning it had unexpected side effects. He was one of them. I was driving it through Reading, still new and glittering, when I found myself somehow in the wrong traffic lane. His Jaguar had pulled up alongside; I tapped the window, and asked politely if he would allow me to cross in front.

He did what in the language he had adopted would be called a double-take. In fact, triple or quadruple might be nearer the mark. Next evening he called me.

I hadn't heard from him for years. He needed artwork, urgently. I didn't trouble too much over the psychology. It was pretty obvious anyway; and after all, a job was a job.

The porch light comes on. He advances grandly, brandishing his slip of paper. Then a surprising thing happens. He approaches my door, only to change course abruptly. He runs to the driver's side; back to me, and round again. I'm baffled for a moment; then understanding dawns, with a species of shock. He's trying to see Lemady's face; but each time she turns away, presents him with a tumble of blonde hair. He was always easy to read; like one of the gundogs he favors, to enhance his image as a country squire. When a woman passes, the focus of his eyes alters; and you know you have lost his attention. This is going a little far though, even for him. Nor was it pre-arranged; I would never have thought of such a thing. Lemady has though, and fast.

Years later I am to see the savage film *Mondo Cane*, a catalogue of the brutal things men do to each other, to animals and occasionally themselves. At one point, a speedboat with scantily-clad girls on board circles a U.S. flat-top at her moorings. A helicopter films the result; the wave of men rushing from side to side of the great deck each time the boat appears. I experience the same cold thrill. So this is the Dominant Male, in action. It doesn't look very dominant to me.

I'm sitting in a pub in Waitrose-on-Thames. At the moment, the digs I have are just over the hill. I've got into the habit of dropping the barmaid home. She's a pretty, vivacious girl who lives a few hundred yards along the road.

The ex-employer appears; with a flourish, like the Kanaka Lover in the tired old Ketèlbey piece. His attention is engaged at once. When the girl asks if her lift will be OK tonight, he enquires where she lives.

"Just down the road. It's all right, Keith will see to it."

His eyes have begun to gleam. "I'm going that way myself. It's on my way. I can take you...."

She glances at us both, with no detectable expression. "I don't give a damn who takes me, as long as I get there."

He scrabbles in his pocket for a coin. "Then it's between us it seems. Come on; call....

I withdraw, mentally. "Sam, this gentleman seems to want to drive you home." I ask her next day if there were any problems. She shakes her head. "No, none at all." She looks thoughtful. "What a peculiar man."

"You have to make allowances. He's a genius." Which must be right; he says so himself finally, in the local paper. Though since he's paying for the ad, I suppose he can put what copy he likes.

A psychologist would perhaps have interesting remarks to make about us both. I refuse to sink to his level; he has to score at any price, in things both large and small. I know him well enough by now; but there's still a sense of uneasiness. He's like a truly alien color, coming from the dark.

Such things are not uncommon. Sometimes they shock by unexpectedness. The pub Lemady and I walk into, that warm summer evening, offers a surprise to us both. The exterior is pebbledashed, finished in a sad pale green; the bar is wide and welcoming, massively timbered. I down my shandy gratefully. As we are leaving, she nods to a dusty glass case, mounted on the wall. "What's in that?"

"I don't know. I can't see properly."

I peer. A tiny, slit-eyed face manifests itself between skeins of cobweb. The lips are drawn back in a centuries-old grimace. *Found in the roof space during renovations*, reads a handwritten card. *In the Middle Ages small animals were often sealed into new buildings to ensure their future luck. May we suggest a large whisky?* On the road, Lemady wails formally. It's a threnody for the long-dead kitten.

We're in a hotel in the Cotswolds. We're too late for a meal; but they've agreed to do sandwiches. A plateful appears. They look good.

"There you are. Get stuck in."

No answer. Lemady's face has paled; she is staring fixedly at the corner of the room. I follow her glance. There's nothing there of course.

I touch her arm. "Are you all right?"

She comes round with a start. "Yes. I'm sorry...."

"What were you looking at? What did you see?"

She shivers. "It doesn't matter. Don't ask me again. I shall never tell you." She starts in on the sandwiches, with a sort of determined enthusiasm.

We're sitting in a tent, looking out at the Purbecks. It's a fine evening; we'll go down to the village soon, to the pub that in a curious way she has made her own. She enjoys her visits now; sometimes even suggests them. The regulars are unfailingly polite.

She speaks suddenly. "I do love you, Keith. It wouldn't matter if you were disabled or something. You know, stuck in a wheelchair. I'd still look after you."

"What on earth made you say that?"

She looks puzzled. "I don't know."

"It wasn't your Sight thing again, was it?"

She shakes her head. "No. At least, I don't think so. It was just something that came to me."

Mercifully, the contingency is not to arise. I wouldn't want her running round after a cripple; it would be a waste of her life.

The phenomenon of Second Sight seems much believed in by the Celts; or at least, those who claim Celtic roots. Lemady produces a curious little book. As a lad, the author worked for a relative on a boat that plied between the Scottish mainland and the Western Isles. One night as he is preparing for sleep, he is startled by a clanging from the hold. The older man reassures him.

"It's all right. Tomorrow we shall be asked to carry a coffin. Don't worry about it."

The coffin duly appears. A burial party accompanies it. As the men embark, they throw their shovels aboard. The sound repeats itself. I'm not sure what that should be called; Second Hearing presumably. I don't accept such notions without question, seductive though they might appear; and useful though they certainly are to fantasists in search of instant plots. But neither do I reject them out of hand. It's the business of negative proof again.

Telepathy, telekinesis, and the like suffer similar drawbacks. Experimental data are invariably unsatisfactory; though a poltergeist manifestation I heard about once certainly fulfilled the classic criteria. While I have seen it claimed that a single human brain contains more circuits than all the computers ever built; up to a few years ago anyway. The estimate is dubious to say the least; but the potential is obviously considerable. A Movieola I once worked with had the habit of picking up police messages and the intercoms of aircraft, not now and then but in a steady stream; it made it all but impossible to use. A Movieola is a simple device for viewing prints as they come back from the labs; my particular specimen had a single stage amp, and of course no aerial or detector circuit. The sound man changed a couple of resistors and capacitors, and the nuisance ceased. He couldn't be specific about what he had done; but the resonance had altered. If such a basic machine could function as a receiver, it would be strange if the mass of circuitry we carry between our ears didn't pick up the odd spurious signal, proceeding from who knows where; it's an expression of normality rather than the reverse. It's the way Sensitives operate perhaps; while at its most commonplace level, most of us from time to time feel what for want of a better term we call an atmosphere. Buildings, locations, seem "friendly" to us, or the reverse. Though doubtless, many factors are involved. Our mood, to start with; and that in turn depends on a host of things. It's impossible to dissect individual strands, lay them out neatly for examination.

My world would seem to have consisted of bars of various sorts. Again, there are two answers to this. They form part of the lifestyle of some bachelors at least, and a fair few business folk. A lot of deals are done over a drink, a lot of friendships made; I first met my long-term colleague Peter Pearce in a hotel in Maidenhead. The second point is more deliberate. Lemady's most private moments have remained exactly that. By definition, they didn't take place in front of witnesses; hence the succession of public locations. In a way, I feel the same about the characters I wrote down; Molly, Kaeti, and a good few more. They have a right to secrets of their own.

There's perhaps a third reason. At teatimes in particular, Lemady usually heads determinedly for the nearest hotel. In her experience they do the cheapest cuppa; and you can enjoy it in reasonable surroundings. It's another example of her unerring practicality.

As for the rest; there's still a feeling, unspoken but widespread, that pubs are somehow dens of Nameless Vice. A relic of Victorian times perhaps; our forefathers were strong on moral values. There was another aspect of course. While folk were enjoying themselves, they weren't making profit for their masters. Faith without works—in this case the works of others—is notoriously dead.

Christina sums it up memorably. She's a Polish girl of startling beauty; I meet her by chance in of all places, a pub in Waitrose-on-Thames. She's on holiday with her husband, a burly young

Master Baker from Solihull. She looks round her, at the crimson upholstery and all the rest. When she first came to England, she would not enter such places.

"Why was that?"

She asks me solemnly if I know what the phrase "public house" means in her language.

"You tell me."

She giggles. "Is brossel. But now...I know they not."

"Not as a rule. Some might be I suppose. But I don't know of any."

She tells me she is very happy here. Which is obvious enough. Right now though there is one thing she badly wants.

"What's that?"

She looks thoughtful. "It is silly. A book in Polish. I would like to read my own language again."

"That sounds easy enough."

Apparently it has not proved so. They went to London yesterday; but not even Foyles could supply her need. Textbooks abounded; but it was not a textbook she wanted.

"You mean fiction. A novel, something like that."

"Yes. A novel. Then it would seem...for a little while I would be at home again."

"Don't go away," I say. "I think I can maybe help."

The digs are only over the road. I hurry across. Some time before, I had had an unusual request. A Polish publisher wanted to do *The Boat of Fate*. Payment would be in zlotys; but there was just one snag. I couldn't get them out of the country; at least, not without penal deductions. If I wished it though, an account would be opened for me in the Bank Handlowy in Warsaw. For all I know, it may still be there. I agreed, but on one condition. They weren't to run the zlotys on wire netting; it makes their feet sore. It probably caused a certain amount of confusion in my agent's foreign sales department.

To my faint surprise, a couple of copies had turned up only a day or so before. They were poorly produced, by our standards at least; the backs coarsely glued, and bound in what looked to be sugar paper. But at least the thing exists. I take one back, and sign it. Christina is delighted. She riffles the pages; then her eyes widen. She has just noticed the author name. "You...*write*?" she says disbelievingly. "You...*write*...."

Wow. But even us backstreet hacks get the occasional bonus.

I tell my colleague about the strange coincidence. "When you think about it, I don't suppose there are all that many who could have done that. Not even in Waitrose-on-Thames."

He looks thoughtful, as is his wont. "I don't suppose there are all that many in the country."

I expect he's right. Not that it's of critical importance to me. I imagine the sort of fanfares other folk would sound though. People like my ex-employer. But a natural law seems to be involved. The ones who've done the job aren't the ones who shoot their mouths off; they leave that for the rest. In any case I've had my reward. I gave a copy to a beautiful expatriate; it's all I really care about.

I had a job once with a nasty little sweatshop in Surrey. Predictably, after eighteen months I got the boot. It was for extracting the cash from them for a freelance animation job they pushed me into with a friend; but that's another matter. I tell the studio manager, a quiet, humorous man who went through World War Two as a WOP/AG on Lancs. He marches me out to his favored local; an odd little place, long since demolished, that in those days was the farthest outpost for the Waitrose-on-Thames Brewery. He sips in silence for a while; then he turns. "Tell me," he says, "have you ever seen your best friend's head bounce down an aircraft fuselage, with a surprised look on its face?"

"Obviously the answer's no. What happened?"

They had drawn the short straw; the Rhine, with its massive defenses. What the aircrews used to call Happy Valley. A close shell burst slammed the door from the flight deck. His pal was coming through it at the time. He was decapitated.

I consider. He's a fund of stories, most of them hilarious. This is the first time he has spoken of anything like this.

"Why did you tell me, Tom? Why now?"

He sets his jaw. "You know Brian chucked his notice. This leaves me with nobody on the advertising side." He drinks ale. "I lost some good mates in the War. I stayed alive. See what I had to come back to."

"I'm sorry."

"I'll survive," he says. "Gets to be a habit after a time." He drains his glass. "Tip up, you're getting slow. Next one's yours."

"No problem," I say. "Cheers." *Ecce Homo* would somehow seem more appropriate. The jokes are one thing; but this man lived through Hell. Same as the folk on the ground. Just for a moment then the curtain slipped; I glimpsed what lies behind the closed lips, the wary, friendly eyes. He'll be back in the office tomorrow; and the next day, the day after that. Just as friendly, just as urbane; hearing the plotting, the evasions, the half-truths. Hell hasn't ended; it's just that the form has changed. Become more insidious.

Obviously I should have promoted myself more. Joined the ratrace, honed the stiletto; put a red nose on, and danced about at Conventions. After all, what matters is that you're noticed; what people say is secondary. Or at least I could have pushed my characters more,

61

if that wasn't to my taste. In a way it might be said I'd let them down; Molly and all the rest. If I was manic, it would have come easier. Any sort of mania will do; it arrests the wandering attention of editors and the like. But egomania is probably best. It's certainly the most widespread. But I was tired of it even before I started writing; though I hadn't formalized the thought at the time. It had got to be like watching the same old weary film; the only variation was an occasional change in the order of the reels.

There was another factor. A proper training in the arts flattens you, or should. When the pieces join back together, if they ever do, you've realized a basic truth; that the job matters more than you do. I was wrong in a way to take on Illustration. I should have gone for a commercial course, spent my time silvering bits of string, knocking out record sleeves nobody was going to produce. I could have shouted the odds with the rest then, competed on a proper level.

Stella Welles, the little *coloratura* heroine from a piece I did that I called "Missa Privata," goes through that particular hoop. It was another story I was surprised to get into print. My editor of the time pushed the manuscript aside dismissively. "I shan't use that of course."

"I didn't expect you would. Any particular reason?"

He looks at me as if called on to explain something to a singularly obtuse child. "Because *I* don't know anything about music...."

It's the only time I get my way simply by raising an eyebrow. I wish I could have done it more often; it's immensely labor-saving.

Readers of science fiction are, or can be, peculiar folk. Though as ever there are honorable exceptions. In the main, they don't mind gobbledegook; in fact it's preferred. They're quite happy for it not to make sense as long as they're sure it doesn't make sense to anybody else either; that way the ghetto stays intact.

The phenomenon once called cyber-punk is a case in point. Reading an example, or trying to, I find myself going back to the start; like Bach beginning again on that mysteriously unplayable score. Each sentence is like a Möbius strip; those harmless twists of paper that have been the excuse for so many bad plots. (And some extremely good ones of course). An enthusiast explains the paradox. "You wouldn't understand," he says grandly. "It's partly Computer Language...." Later the originator, a personable and obviously shrewd young man who has "made a lot of money"—the standard phrase used by those who wish to suggest superior knowledge, but in fact have no idea—observes mildly that there is a degree of satire involved. His audience laughs, a little hesitantly. The shadow of the King's new clothes doesn't seem all that far away; but that can be disregarded. After all, the fairy tale is written in plain language; so it lacks a proper significance.

The ghetto-forming impulse seems a widespread human trait. Leastways, the urge to invest the obvious with an air of arcane mystery, which effectively comes to the same thing. A favorite story of the composer Vaughan Williams was of the time when, leaving the hall after the *première* of one of his many folk operas, he overheard a conversation between two old trouts. "Charming piece," said the first. "Quite delightful...."

"Yes," agreed her friend judicially. "Pity it wasn't in its original language though...."

A friend of mine, who happens to be a top man in the field of microprocessors, and apparently a good deal beside—I didn't know how revered he was till the prayer mats started coming out at mention of his name—is buttonholed by a computer buff. "What I want to do, you see," he explains portentously, "is access a sophisticated language...."

My friend, who has very evidently come out for a quiet ale rather than to trade high-speed jargon, looks pained. "Try English," he suggests. The horse's mouth, it seems, has struck again.

Fashions come and go; in the science fiction market, the old staples remain. Pretty girls are flung from spaceships, as excess to the payload; Shakespeare/Anne Boleyn/Old King Cole saves the world from nuclear war. An aniline-tinted shutter seems to drop in front of such pieces, like the filters the movie people used to isolate the fantasy world of "Bali Hai." The readers get tired and move on; but there are always fresh ones coming along. And markets are there to be supplied.

Paul Eulenstein, the old maestro who is Stella's mentor, tells her a story. "When I am touring, I will not conduct the same piece twice in any town. They come to me and say, 'The subscribers will be different tomorrow, everyone in the hall. Everyone!' But I am cunning, I do not believe. I think, perhaps one, just one, has come again! He has slipped in past the door! He will hear me again, and the music will not be new. And he will think, 'He is not a clever man at all but rather a silly one, who wears too-bright bow ties!'"

Real life is harder to handle though. And anyway the old man is not being wholly ingenuous. He is spinning words, to put the girl who is to become his protégée more at her ease.

The old saying about the good wine and the bush doesn't necessarily hold true. It may have done in Roman times; though that seems open to doubt as well. As an adman I knew it anyway. Most of my work fell into the trade category; the vast majority of accounts do. The glamourous consumer schemes most folk seem to think of automatically, including from time to time the media pundits themselves, are a thin icing on a large and very varied cake. If person A has made a superior mouse trap, and person B doesn't know, then he or she has no chance of buying it. The idea is to spread the information, as widely and economically as possible; it's as unglamourous and vital as that. It was how Kerosina Books were launched; though I've no doubt that before they took to their collective heels, alarmed at their unwanted success, the Board put it down in some mysterious way to their own magnetic presence.

If success is achieved, the advertising man is often its first victim. The client will attribute the improved sales to his own genius and the brilliance of his product, and not infrequently fires his Agency as surplus to requirements. A modest increase is safest to aim for; but that is not easy to secure. The process tends to be all or nothing.

Sometimes the displeasure is visited more immediately. I was involved once in devising a scheme to attract unqualified school leavers into a nationalized industry. Previous attempts, via the *Times* and the *Telegraph*, had met with signal lack of response.

I conferred sadly with my colleague of the time. We suggested schedules be drawn up for the tabloids; late developers could scarcely be expected to be searching the top staff columns for jobs. I would have thought that was obvious to a dolt; but apparently it had not been so to the client. A day or so after the ads appeared, our revered employer turned up in a temper. He had received a furious phone call from Town. They were only offering half a dozen places; but the response had been in thousands. The office had been thrown into confusion; a special department had had to be set up to process the jam. The lesson learned by Meadow Sutcliffe so many years before had been administered again.

Before that's seen as a piece of special pleading for the glories of privatization, my colleague once took a comma to Birmingham, that it might be examined by the Board. The Company concerned was large, world famous and highly Limited. The punctuation had been inserted, on their instructions, in the headline of an ad: but a final decision was apparently impossible at a distance, despite having both versions of the copy in front of them. They had to see the thing itself. Commas of course are a vital part of the writer's armory, or should be; I would be the last to decry them. After all, it was the presence or absence of a pause mark in the ancient statute defining traitorous conduct that hung Roger Casement and buried him in lime. He was going to be topped anyway, as a matter of principle; or revenge, depending on the viewpoint. But it was punctuation that finally sealed his fate. In my colleague's case, the addition made no difference whatever to the sense.

I once wrote a story from the viewpoint of a slow-witted lavatory attendant. In fact I wrote two; I found the situation rich in possibilities. Allowing a little necessary licence, as such a man could scarcely be expected to be keeping a written diary, I decided to allow him limited knowledge of punctuation. Full stops and commas only;

the use of semicolons would be beyond his mental means. The result had a rushing, breathy quality that added greatly to its drama. It was taken on without too much trouble by an American fantasy magazine. No proofs were forthcoming of course; at that level, one scarcely looks for such refinements. When a copy of the thing finally turned up, my rage knew no bounds. Somebody, either a sub or the editor himself, had corrected the text. All semicolons had been lovingly and correctly replaced; I had received a lesson in punctuation. For the first and only time, I longed for the return of the quicklime and the rope. I understand the process is sovereign for concentrating the mind.

There is another aspect to the curious business of advertising that is perhaps less generally appreciated, at least by those who have not been involved. Before a scheme has a chance to do its job, it has to be sold to the advertiser himself. Which is frequently the hardest part. Though for the most part the account executive, so-called, doesn't bother; just comes back and kicks the visualizer. His only recourse is to kick the office cat, if it can be found.

Some clients are superb of course; a privilege to meet and work with. Others are less so. If the man behind the desk gets stroppy, the best ploy is to persuade him he thought of the idea himself and hope he rests on his laurels.

If his creativity can be kept at bay, there's a chance we can make some money for him. The same goes for the copy of course. Kaeti says somewhere that if an amateur puts one word after the next, you can be sure of one thing. The second word will be wrong. There's no certainty about the first one either of course; but she was being charitable.

I suffered an account exec once who fancied himself as a creative man. His crowning effort was for the promotion of a local toy fair. *"Sorry, parents,"* ran the giggling headline. The theme was elaborated at length. One visit, and the family would be broke. No money left for Christmas puds, mince pies, turkeys; the list was extensive. Nothing had been omitted; I was fascinated by what seemed the ultimate in anti-sells. But the studio manager was jerked for once from his habitual apathy. "Christ, we can't run this...." He took it to the head of the company, an austere Victorian relic who at least had the virtue of sound common sense. A distant explosion, and the matter was resolved.

Though kitsch can have its own esoteric pleasures. I'm given the job of promoting a range of garden tools. Looking through the list, I'm struck by their lethal nature. What we need to do is dress a girl in black leathers, hang the armoury about her; the murderous machine saws and machetes, flamethrowers for the subjugation of weeds. The copy angle likewise suggests itself. *"There was disaffection in the flower beds; the vegetable patch was suspected of non-alignment...."*

But the client recoils. No; best have a set of little boxes like last time, show each device with its list number. It will be safer.

It will certainly be safer for the Agency. The ad will lose itself obligingly among its competitors; sales-wise, the middle course will be achieved.

Hmm. Black leathers. I once supplied a copy of James Elroy Flecker's unique and startling play *Hassan* to a young woman of memorable beauty who was currently performing a variety of unmemorable tasks for a local amateur dramatic outfit; one for which in fact I had a good deal of regard. I'd got onto moderately good terms with her some time before, as a result of a discussion about casting the parts for an upcoming musical production. I observed that if it lay with me she would lead every show, at which she looked faintly blank. "But you haven't heard me sing," she said. "You might not like my voice." There was of course only one answer to be made. "Girl, don't be irrelevant." Later, I consolidated myself in her good books. Another of their shows was scheduled for the local theatre. Discussing it with a friend in the pub across the road, I said I hoped this time she had got a decent part. "They need to look after her better than they do. She's Celtic, after all; they're not all that thick on the ground round here."

"What gives you that idea?" asked a remembered voice. So the advance party was already here; she had stood beside me listening to the exchange, presumably with a degree of interest.

I was fairly caught; so it was a case of in for a penny, in for a pound. "Facial beauty of course, great bone structure; graceful hands and arms (for once it was true), superb eyes, high intelligence; shall I go on?" She looked reflective, then smiled. "You'd better come to the show." I did, and never regretted it; I hadn't really needed to be shamed into attending.

She was Celtic, by the way; Welsh, on her mother's side. She admitted it later, to my vast relief. As for the leathers; I saw her as Pervaneh, girlfriend of the leader of the dissidents. Both meet fearsome deaths at the hands of Flecker's monstrous Caliph. I would dress her as a modern gun girl, complete with M16; all freedom fighters are terrorists as well, it just depends which side ef the fence you happen to be sitting. For the ghost scene, I would have costumed her in white; pathetically, her gun would have been white too. Oh, well.... Moral, stay with the written page. It causes less hassle; though truth to tell, there's sometimes not a sight to choose between.

I feel a certain empathy for Meadow Sutcliffe. Sometimes one gets ahead of the field by accident; at others the temptation is too strong to resist. The local Co-Op announces the imminent arrival of Santa Claus. He's doing it in style this year, by Viking long boat. Mercifully I'm not called on to witness the event; I stay in the back room with my drawing board. The war galley with its threatening figurehead crashes handsomely from a half page upright, appalling the boss's son. Such a thing might frighten the children, as it has already frightened him. Where, he seems to be asking, are the scratchy little thumbnails he is used to, spattered coyly across a standard comp's layout? He forgives me though; partially at least. "It's a funny thing, Roberts," he announces grandly. "These drawings of yours. The crudity puts you off to start with; but you get quite used to it...." I feel moderately reprieved. He'll fire me eventually of course; everybody has to get their kicks somehow, and I've felt for some time sacking people helps him with erections. But for the moment all would seem to be sweetness and light.

There is a certain irony involved. The grossly ignorant might well be unassailable; but neither can they insult efficiently. By definition, they don't know enough. "Roberts is a very bad artist," observes a fan reviewer judicially. "It's strange though how his drawings always seem to suit their subjects." Exactly the same was said about Tenniel, the original illustrator of *Alice in Wonderland*; so I'm in august company indeed. "What you've got to realize," says an unpleasant hanger-on, intent, for his own reasons, on causing trouble if possible, "is that Kaeti has no more reality than an Edwardian chorine." I'm tempted momentarily to ask him to put it in writing. Shades of *La Belle Epoque*, the great Alphonse Mucha; I'm positively uplifted. I don't bother though; something about artificial pearls, and real swine. Also of course the wasting of one's breath.

My long-term colleague is a master of the art of ego massage. It makes both our lives easier. Though his technique mostly takes the form of masterly inaction. In some ten or twelve years we only have a couple of jobs turned down flat; which ought to be worth an entry in the *Guinness Book of Records*. I even practice the craft myself from time to time, when I'm in the mood and when I can be bothered. A babble of suggestions greets my request for a copyline for the bookplate that is to launch Kerosina's first production. I seize on one.

"That's brilliant. Absolutely what we need. I really think it would work...."

The originator glows with pleasure. I think he has a genuine hot flush, whatever they might be. He has contributed; he has been creative. But of course he's a very creative person; even I was finally forced to admit it. He could easily have written *Kaeti & Company* himself, had he not been occupied with more important matters.

In fact it's a useful line; it was one of several possibilities I had in mind. What he has actually done is quote from the text; but the penny hasn't dropped. Nor do I suppose it will. I doubt he'll open the book again; he'll be too busy soaking up the plaudits, real or imaginary, for having become a Captain of Industry.

Doris Lessing could have taken her comments further. She didn't; having a precise mind, she answered what she had been asked, and stopped. She's no stranger though to the brainless ways of publishers. Not all that long ago she insisted on one of her manuscripts being offered under pseudonym. Quite obviously, her agent would have been annoyed. Instead of trotting down the road and coming back with a healthy contract, he or she was going to have to do a fair amount of thankless work.

A considerable amount, as it transpired. The thing floated about for a year or more, getting the thumbs-down from reader after reader, before receiving a microscopic advance from the States. I would have been covered with confusion had I been one of the many to commit the gaffe, but publishers' minds don't function that way. No doubt they were irritated by what they would consider gross unfairness. After all, one ought to be told, loudly and clearly, what one is looking at; it's unreasonable to be asked to use one's taste and judgment. They are busy folk; they have far more important things to do.

I am shown a book designed by a Scottish artist and author. Hands in the margins point to various paragraphs; key numbers indicate whether the reader is to laugh or cry. I'm surprised at first; then I realize what a good idea it is. It's comforting to be told how to react; it would be a boon to reviewers. After all, anything's better than having to think; that hurts.

Lessing was making a serious point of course, though nobody particularly cared. It's what the readers already know that's important; what's passing in front of their eyes is largely irrelevant.

I agree to an unpublished novella being used as a subject for a writers' workshop in Glasgow; something I would normally avoid like the plague, but for once I feel I have no option. The request was made by a friend who runs the group as part of the University's extramural program; he was more than helpful during the writing of the piece, to refuse would have been churlish in the extreme. As a faint salve, I detail exactly what will be said and send him a checklist. Later he mails me a tape of the session. He agrees wryly I was correct at all points. Strangers spending a few days in the city and imagining they know it; suspect, outdated slang, and so on. All the comments recorded were made by Glaswegians with whom I had talked, I was careful to add none of my own; while the slang was drawn from a dubious little booklet produced by the Central Libraries Committee, and sold in large numbers to the tourists. To make the point plain I even had one of my characters wave the offending pamphlet about; but that passed undetected. The readers had already decided what they would find; the text itself was surplus to requirements.

Reading, or the specialized variation used by those retained by publishers for the lowly task, is an interesting process. The rate used to be fifty bob a manuscript; it has probably gone up a little but I doubt by much, so speed is obviously essential. Various methods are employed; a popular and quite useful one is to scan the centres of the lines north to south and take in every tenth page complete. Enough can be gleaned to fill in the form supplied. The contents of such documents are kept a closely guarded secret, at least from such potentially disruptive elements as authors. When I asked an editor of my acquaintance if he would show me one, he refused. Asked why, his answer was blunt; he didn't want his office broken up.

During my time in Waitrose-on-Thames I became intrigued by a middle-aged lady who had a cottage just along the road. Saturday afternoons were her time for earning pin money. She would dispose herself on the front room carpet, a stack of manuscripts to one side, a gin bottle and a vast ashtray on the other; she had obviously been doing the job for some time, because her speed was truly awesome. Peering through the window, I would watch the flicking of the pages with disbelief. A well-known fantasy writer once described a pair of publishers, forced by some contingency to read and judge all the entries for a novel competition in a day, dosing themselves with various stimulants and as a result getting high as kites. I have news that will maybe disappoint his readers; the sequence was based more or less on fact. But then, most good fantasy is; it always used to be said, the surest way to be disbelieved was to tell the truth.

I once spent a few days with friends on the amazing Shropshire Union Canal; "the Shroppie," beloved of narrow boat enthusiasts. The endless sombre cuttings with their exotic micro-climates had a strange mental effect. As a result, I wrote a story set on a far planet. A short time later I was amazed to get a note from the then editor of *The Butty*, organ of the already long-established Society restoring the Kennet and Avon. He had much enjoyed the piece, and felt his readers would too. Could he run it in the magazine?

Fiction in *The Butty*; whatever next? But I suppose that has to count as another first.

There was an even more curious sequel. I received a nicely-produced handbook on the huge Pennsylvania complex, from the President of the American Canal Society; I hadn't even known such a body existed. He would like to do an SF collection of realistic canal stories; but mine and a companion piece were the only ones he had found. All he had managed to come up with otherwise was an Edgar Rice Burroughs story where the canals of Mars were fed from the polar ice caps, and flowed to the equator by gravity. In which again, one seems to detect some sort of moral.

The joke inherent in the situation is fairly patent of course. How many folk reading the stories who didn't realize they were so

Earth-based, not to say earthy, can't be known; what is certain is that anybody from the English canal fraternity, coming across them by chance, would wonder what the hell descriptions of the Shroppie were doing in the middle of a book that purported to be SF.

What may also seem a little odd is that after maintaining stoutly that I never wrote SF, thoughts of the genre have never been far away. The truth is of course that for many years all short fiction was genre fiction. SF and fantasy had their strictures; and over the years they got tighter, in spite of countless enthusiastic claims. But compared with, say, crime, horror, ghost, romantic, to name but four, SF was still a fairly broad church. The name of the game, as far as I was concerned, was to masquerade; and I'll cheerfully own up to it. I seemed to suit a fair few people along the way though; so in the main the results maybe weren't wholly bad.

On the other hand, an old witticism has it that certain of the American magazines had turned science fiction into a branch of *Popular Mechanics*. Maybe in my own small way, I was trying to do the same.

Literary values, whatever they might be, can obviously be argued over, or ducked behind, more or less endlessly. My preference has always been for writers who made no such dizzy claims. I read Gerald Durrell's first book at a sitting, which is more than I can say for the output of his illustrious brother. In later years, James Herriot delighted me. The writing was engaging, unpretentious, and obviously backed by a lifetime of experience. But the former point recurs at once. I believe the first manuscript was submitted a couple of dozen times; the author was about to give up when it was taken on, grudgingly I'm prepared to bet and with a degree of patronage. The subject had been handled before of course, without conspicuous success; there is always a degree of uncertainty in such things, despite the trumpeting of the hype specialists. But anybody who couldn't see that what they had, potentially at least, was *Doctor in the House* with a leg at each corner, needed their brain examining, if such an organ could be discovered at all.

I was once guilty of an extreme lapse of judgment myself; though I think I can justifiably claim extenuating circumstances. While staying with him in Silverdale, Bon unexpectedly thrusts a wad of yellow typescript at me. "Read it," he commands imperiously.

"What, now? There's an awful lot of it. What is it...."

I turn to the title page, and do a double-take. *Don't Point That Thing at Me*, by Kyril Bonfiglioli. I do my best to become involved; but with the author standing over me, pulling faces like the Knight of Bushido I remember from the corner of his Oxford study, it's next to impossible. Finally he snatches the thing away. "You're not laughing! You don't think it's funny! *You're not laughing*...." Nor did I for a year or more, till I sat with the published book in my lap. Bon's own hands decorated the wrapper, cocking a nine mil. semi-automatic. Least, I think they were; he certainly owned a pistol that was a dead ringer. Then, the text exploded on me as well. Okay, so it was built round Geoffrey Household's famous thriller *Rogue Male*. Not surprising; Bon had always been a Household fan. Borrowing isn't important; everything has been written before anyway. It's what you do with the borrowings that counts. After all, if you must fly to extremes, Shakespeare never thought up a single plot. Not far into the book the protagonist, an art dealer (what else) instructs his restorer to clean some later retouching from an eighteenth-century Venus; he suspects the drapery of concealing a particularly fine example of the Nun's Wink. Later, a sort of female Bismarck orders the hero to her daughter's bedroom. "There will be time to couple before dinner...." Household was never like this.

"Murderously witty" proclaimed the blurb. The panel thought so too when they gave it their award for Crime Novel of the Year. It summed it up pretty fairly; I suppose it would sum Bon up as well.

I am to try a pseudonymous approach. *The Road to Paradise*, my last title with Kerosina, had in fact been written some twelve years before. I use a byline from the old days, when Ted Carnell, my first editor, was still gleefully soaking up my slushpile. I have a very specific reason. It has come to me, perhaps belatedly, that it might be an idea to dump the sf label, with all its implications. If that means dumping my name as well, so be it. This is a mainstream book, in so far as such a thing can be defined; so it seems as good a time as any.

The result is curious. A while later my agent, an excellent and long-suffering man, calls me. He will have to blow the cover; right now, the Establishment is not prepared to consider submissions from unknowns.

I agree. A year or so on, he asks me to look through the sheaf of rejections. Normally we have an understanding about that. Part of his job is to absorb such things. I have enough to keep me busy without being distracted by constant vituperation. But in this case he has a reason too.

The objections fall under two main headings. Keith Roberts, "author of *Pavane*," cannot possibly handle this sort of material; also, the story has a murder in it. It is therefore a thriller; so why doesn't it read like Ed McBain? The pigeonhole mentality was one thing; this is the straitjacket.

It's obvious to the meanest wit, or should be, the art of insurance is the art of not paying cash out if it can be avoided; the less the company coughs up, the happier the shareholders. What is not so generally appreciated is that the art of publishing is the art of not producing books. When a manuscript does crawl into print it's another story; the wheeling and dealing can begin, the cake, if any, can be sliced up to the satisfaction of all concerned. Except the author of course, but that's another matter. He or she has already received their reward; the honor and glory of the printed page. Until such happy time though the thing is a dangerous unknown quantity, about which somebody has to make a decision. So there are a thousand cast-iron reasons for turning it down. I could have thought of loads more reasons for bouncing *Road*, had my job depended on it; the unanimity didn't indicate the genius of the trade in divining the book's weak points, merely the threadbare nature of its imagination.

The thing worked to my advantage in the end of course. I was enabled to do my own production and promotion, a job on which my colleague Mr. Pearce collaborated more than ably. Essentially, a book is an exercise in packaging; between us we had a half century of experience, so we were able to be "artistic" to effect. *Ars celare artem.*

It's perfectly possible to sell ice cream to Eskimos of course, given one thing; they like the taste. For a couple of decades, in common no doubt with most other writers, I had suffered a nagging insinuation; each book was issued from the kindness of the publishers' hearts, if they didn't take it nobody else would. The old capitalist ploy in fact, as the process was once defined to me. Though patently nonsensical—if any one title had failed to go into the black the shutters would have gone up fast enough—continual dripping had had an undeniable effect. The speed with which the Special Edition of *Kaeti & Company* was oversubscribed rapidly put paid to that; within a very short time the book itself had become rare. The same was true of other titles produced by Kerosina; in the early days at least, before the inevitable hubris led to overproduction.

The other factor of course affecting any limited edition operation is distribution. Would the existing network of specialist dealers and collectors prove adequate? Particularly in England, where it seemed the majority of sales would be made? Here of course my colleague and I could help with targeted promotion; later, as we knew very well, the Company would cease to bother, having, in its own eyes at least, already become world famous. The old pattern would re-establish itself; though as I pointed out at the time, the débâcle came in most respects as a relief. When boats are seen heading at high speed for the horizon, the normal assumption would be that the ship was sinking; in this case, it was because the damned thing refused to.

The effect of packaging is impossible to quantify with exactness; the buyer's instant response to my colleague's wrapper was unusual to say the least. As ever, the designer is at a massive disadvantage. Negative results are only too painfully apparent; the plusses are more evanescent. In any case, in such a project the majority of sales are not made through traditional retail outlets; so presentation is very much the icing on the cake. But a sale is a sale is a sale; the effects are cumulative. Embarrassingly so, as I had already found.

The session we set up for the wrapper and internal shots of *Road to Paradise* is in some ways the strangest part of the job. The model walks into a village pub not far from Salisbury. For a moment I'm afflicted by a sense of multiple realities; the sort of thing I talked about, perhaps glibly, in *Pavane*. After all, when the text was first written this girl was a child. But here she is, finally; not exactly what I had in mind perhaps, but close enough for jazz. Anyway she will add a color of her own; that's what it's all about.

I feel I have to try at least to rise to the occasion. The character she will be playing is a young author, well-connected. So it's best to pitch in at the deep end.

"May I present the Honorable Maggie Blighe?"

My colleague murmers something appropriate. But then, he's in the spirit of the occasion already. It's the sort of thing that doesn't need spelling out; to him at least.

We move the model outside for the frontispiece shot. It's to be the last of the session. She has warmed up beautifully; my colleague has correspondingly slackened pace. As ever, I have been taking my cues from him.

He hangs a camera round the ersatz Maggie's neck. When she first appears in the book she is taking pictures at a Civil War re-enactment. The model looks at the prop thoughtfully. "What do you want me to be now?"

What I want her to be is Calamity Jane; self-confident, maybe a little brash. She has yet to see murder done; time later for the guilt and self-doubt to start. I look round. The vista of fields climaxes with the huge image of the Cathedral.

"You're a great lady, you own everything you can see. So sucks-boo to men."

She draws herself up. "This sort of thing?

Peter is already going for a low viewpoint. But then, I knew he would. Again, it didn't need spelling out.

"*Quel beau visage intelligent*," says a French friend in delight. But all women worthy of the name are actresses at heart. It's part of their psyche, if it can only be tapped. I asked her to be a Goddess for a while; so a Goddess she became. Lemady would understand perfectly well. After all, she would do exactly the same herself.

Packaging has been the downfall of a good many writers, though in the nature of things they couldn't be expected to admit it. Or for the most part maybe appreciate the point. Leaving matters of taste aside, to slap a soft porn cover onto a book that hasn't earned it is to doom it. The teenagers with low reading skills at whom it's presumably aimed, if one can ascribe intention to a process that's largely automatic, will put it back on the shelf in disgust when they hit the first difficult-looking word; people who might get something from it are repelled by the presentation. The author loses both ways; also the publishers, if they had the wit to see it. But they don't. If low sales result, it must be the writer's fault. It can't be anything to do with them; after all, they're experts.

A friend in Amesbury has the last word on that. "An ex is a has-been," he observes. "A spurt is a drip under pressure." Which seems to sum things up nicely.

In other respects, his conclusions are equally brisk. In my first book, *The Furies*, the sf subject that caused so much subsequent confusion, kingsize wasps wreak havoc among the general population. How could they really be dealt with? Bombing and gassing would cause more problems than they solved; while nukes are of course out of the question. There ought to be an answer though; the problem has been at the back of my mind for years. In his Army career, my friend was an artilleryman; latterly he worked on missiles. I put the thing to him. How would he cope?

He looks thoughtful. "You say they can't be gassed?"

"I shouldn't think so. At least, not without doing away with everybody else as well. They're all over the place."

He considers again. "I think...I'd be on the first boat to Calais."

Well, I asked for a professional opinion; and I got it. So maybe the plot wasn't as badly flawed as I had thought.

The man, or woman, who has done the job is really the only one to ask. The experts can add their whiffs of vapor later on. In my one and only thriller, the murder at the Civil War battle is a case in point. It seemed to me there would be a good chance of the killer getting away; after all, there would be bodies scattered everywhere. One more wouldn't be noticed.

It's hardly a new idea of course. An Oriental proverb has it that the best place to hide a pebble is on the beach; while in one of the Father Brown stories a General conceals a murder by staging a battle on the scene. Nonetheless, I consult a policeman friend. He's CID now; but he did his time on the beat. About twenty years, he told me once.

I won't say he goes pale; but he certainly becomes thoughtful. "Christ, you do pick 'em, don't you?"

"You reckon he'd get away with it then?"

"Not much doubt. At the time anyway. There'd probably only be a man on the carpark. If he was dead keen he might set up a murder log on the spot; it's any officer's right. But odds on he wouldn't. Probably be an older bloke anyway, they don't like making those sort of waves."

So that's all right. Maggie's saga can begin.

Most folk are pleased to talk about their jobs. Occasionally one meets suspicion and distrust; but it's fairly rare. A local Red Cross worker supplies further essential facts. She asks for details of the injuries sustained in the shooting Maggie witnesses perforce. I tell her, and she pulls a face. There's little really that could be done. Attempt to control the hemorrhage; turn the victim into the standard recovery position, and so on. Over and above basic knowledge, an old-fashioned quality is called for. It's generally called imagination. She has it in plenty; she's able instantly to enter the mind of a trained helper on the scene. I add my notes to the file that's building, on the book that isn't to read like Ed McBain; a writer of course for whom I have every respect. This is England though, not America. I would have thought the fact self-evident; but of course, I'm not an expert.

Before the text goes for setting, one of the Kerosina meddlers casually alters certain basic facts. I correct the interference; gritting my teeth, because I've never made an author change in my life. I had equipped myself with up-to-date census figures for the major towns of Kent; I can only suppose somebody thought they looked wrong. They can't attend to matters of production, which is why among other things *Kaeti & Company* finished up on proofing paper; but by God, they can poke their fingers into everything else. Not that it's important; terminal hubris is already setting in. Nemesis, as usual, will follow in its wake; she's a watchful and ever-busy Goddess.

Occasionally, proof correction can bring its own rarefied pleasures. Kyril Bonfiglioli, who taught me more about the practice of writing than anybody else, always insisted foreign phrases be checked in the *Oxford Dictionary*, the only source he would accept. His concern was whether or not they had been accepted as normal English usage; should they be expressed in italics?

At one point in a story I used the phrase *per capita*. I knew it well enough, or thought I did; but I looked it up on principle. To my delight I found it is technically incorrect; we can only count one head at a time. I changed my text to the singular, and asked the typesetter to follow it exactly. Later, I watched the great man's Biro with fascination as it approached the fatal point. Finally, he raised his eyebrows. It was a favorite expression; it was the one that made him look like Judge Jeffreys.

"You've written *per caput*. I presume you mean *per capita*?"

"No. I mean exactly what I said."

The expression becomes more extreme. "On what authority?"

"The *Concise....*"

I watch his brain go into overdrive. He realizes he's been had; a split second later he roars with laughter. "I don't give a—*beep*—."

He changes the expression, quite properly, to the accepted usage.

A copy-correcting session is one of my earliest memories of Bon; though on that occasion the object of the exercise was a typescript rather than a set of galleys. He turned up in Waitrose-on-Thames one evening with a version of *The Furies*, already slated for its first magazine outing. His girlfriend of the time was in attendance; for her sake he insisted on going out for a meal. He had not dined; though he had obviously partaken well of the preliminaries.

Somewhat against my instincts I had allowed Ted Carnell, my agent of the time, to talk me into giving the job of typing the final draft to a young friend down on her luck. "She's a nice girl, and a good typist. She really needs the money; and she won't charge the earth...." How often have we heard that one before?

The unknown Trilby didn't charge the earth. I would have settled for paying a little more though, and having my verbs left in; some mental quirk had led her to omit about one in four. Always the verbs, strangely enough; the rest of her work was irreproachable. As Bon warmed to the task of restoring coherence to the text, one or other of his whirling arms would knock the growing pile of typescript persistently from the table to the floor. The room in which we were eating was largeish, and a little raw-boned; the floor was cladded with shiny thermoplastic tiles. Each time the stack of quarto swooshed down, a line of sheets spread to the far tables, watched by the incurious eyes of diners. An increasingly expressionless waiter would retrieve them, and return them to the Master. I hope he was given a reasonable *pourboire*; I wouldn't know. I wasn't party to the transaction; I was too busy heading for the door.

Bon, as I am soon to learn, is the master of any situation, however lugubrious. Conveying my Lady Mother in the direction of the High, he pushes a disc into the strange little car-borne record player strapped beneath the dash of his Rolls. "A little music, madam? I trust Verdi is to your taste...." Suitably impressed, the matriarch attempts a lunchtime comeback. She seems blissfully unaware the internal politics of Kettering Maternity Unit are unlikely to take the City of Dreaming Spires by storm. I wish I could say the same.

My time with Bon was also my first experience of the hard facts of an editor's life. Among the outpourings of would-be authors, three themes cropped up with horrid regularity; concealed environments, shaggy God stories, and Shakespeare. No doubt each scribe considered himself, or occasionally herself, dazzlingly original; though in fact the offerings had a stultifying sameness. The first two categories I could understand to an extent; but what the Swan of Avon had done to merit such continuous attention from no-hopers remained a mystery to me.

Bonfiglioli had a fixed principle with regard to such things. Each returned offering must be accompanied by a personal letter, regardless of its quality as prose.

"For heaven's sake, Bon. Why did God invent the rejection slip?"

He would sigh, assume an expression of exaggerated patience. "Keith, each one of these contributors is also a *reader*. They must be treated as solid gold. One day, you'll develop some compassion...."

If there was any compassion going the rounds, I reckoned I was in for a share at least. A letter from an editor, even a lowly assistant, always had an electrifying effect; and back the thing would come, with any suggestions I had felt duty bound to make lovingly incorporated. Never the better for them, and quite often worse. A few such to-ings and fro-ings and the end result was equally predictable. I had led the correspondent on maliciously, encouraged him or her to slave countless hours at the typewriter; and for what? Never, never would they buy *Science Fantasy* again; so we lost our reader anyway. Bon, though, was deaf to reasoned argument.

Except once. One of the Bard-abusers had decided, for reasons that remained obscure, that Will was penning *Richard III* when news came of Kit Marlowe's death in a tavern brawl. It throws him into a transport of delight. "Now is the winter of our discontent," he scribbles exultantly, "Made glorious summer by my rival's death...." It's only later he is persuaded to substitute the glittering second line, that so encapsulates Richard's jealousy and moroseness, sets the stage for the bloody action that is to come. I lay the typescript down.

"Bon, I want a rejection slip."

He elevates his brows. "You know my feelings on that subject. I do *not* expect to have to repeat them."

Nonetheless he does, in detail. I wait till he has finished.

"I understand all that. I want a rejection slip."

His attention is engaged. "For what reason?"

"This fool has cut in half the most elegant pun in the English language. He has left the two ends writhing on the path like a severed worm, and he has stalked on. But that's not the worst. *He doesn't even know he's done it....*"

The great man extends a hand. "Show me...." He reads the offending passage, considers; then he crosses to a large roll-topped desk in the corner of the study. I have never seen it unlocked. He produces a set of keys, slides the front up. Inside, rubber-banded, is a thick wad of rejection slips. There must be a couple of thousand; and I had never even known what they looked like. He removes one, locks the desk again and hands it to me with a flourish. There is style in all things; and he never turns up an opportunity to display it.

I am to see The Desk unlocked just one more time. On that occasion my attention is caught by the stack on stack of paperbacks inside, each with a plain grey wrapper. I pick one up curiously, open it. I'm still standing with it in my hand when Bon walks in. He begins to caper with glee. *"You're reading a dirty book...."*

Not so much reading; arrested by shock would be a better description. The throbbing columns of gristle, and all the rest; for a moment I hadn't even realized what was being talked about. It's a new vocabulary to learn; not that it would take all that long. It's not particularly extensive. "For God's sake, Bon; who do these belong to?"

He names a co-director of one of his many enterprises; a massive, well-set, and wealthy young man who habitually dresses in the finest Donegal tweed. Leastways, he's a scion of a famous and extremely wealthy family.

"You're joking . What the hell does he want them for?"

He shrugs, and locks the desk. "It's his hobby. He takes them to London by the suitcaseful when he's finished with them. They buy them back at half price, and give him another lot...."

So that's the end result of the priciest education money can buy. Well, well, and well again.

Further words fail me. Doubtless though the Bard would have an answer. Or Bonfiglioli of course. After all, the man who once summed up Freud as "That incredibly dirty-minded old Austrian fortune-teller" could have been relied on to add the last word to any situation. Just for once though, he never supplied it.

The author J. B. Priestley, now fashionably derided, wrote an amusing SF story once. He called it "The Grey Ones," a title later adopted by the perpetrator of a minuscule and disastrous fantasy. In the original, the Grey Ones were folk who put a stop to all human endeavor by hedging it round with petty restrictions and objections; the only way you could tell you had met one of them was if after you had left the office, you couldn't remember his face. The parable is obvious enough; but Priestley made his villains more than mindless timeservers. They were agents of an alien intelligence, bent, for their own ends, on the thwarting of human progress. Maybe it's not as way out as it seems.

The first editor of *The Boat of Fate* was an exception to the rule of facelessness. He was a pugnacious man; if he was going to do the job, then he would back his own judgment. If it didn't work out, the company was welcome to fire him. It got the book accepted; but there was an obvious drawback. The same belligerence was extended to the text. He required certain alterations; either I made them as instructed, or there was no deal. Some I was indifferent about; others hurt, because they were wrong. They unbalanced the story, stressed aspects I had been at pains to play down. As ever though, the situation was double-sided.

I cross the carpark, to where Lemady is waiting. We're off on our wanderings again; this time though she's taking her station wagon. Not that the gear we need couldn't be packed into the Spit; it's already been done more than once. But she decided it was time the other motor had a run.

Behind me, the Thames is doing its own sweet thing; and as it happens I have a pile of books under my arm. She regards them thoughtfully. "You shouldn't be doing your sort of job you know. You'd be better off in a College somewhere; I can just see you in the common room."

I've had the same thought myself, the odd time. But the grass is always greener over the hill. In any case, I read the first, unexpurgated version of the C. S. Lewis classic, *That Hideous Strength*. The third part of his trilogy might well have been a letdown for some; but it was a revelation to me. The egoboo, the plotting, the scrambling for position, are much the same on campus; but there if anything the situation would be worse. In the main, one would imagine the opposition would have a degree at least of intelligence. And the History Man has yet to make his appearance on the scene.

I dump the books into the back of the Cambridge. "I dare say you're right. But what the hell. Let's go to Dorset...."

VI.

From time to time, Lemady adopts some striking guises. She's five ten now, and Swedish. The stipulated height for a fashion model; which is exactly what she used to be. She still looks the part. Her blonde hair cascades almost to her classically tiny waist; all in all, she's the schoolboy's dream of home.

Right now her face is far from dreamlike. She's sobbing, fighting for breath; beside herself, in the good old-fashioned phrase. She's just back from the Far East, from a meeting with her husband; an attempt, fruitless it would appear, to patch her marriage up. Her folk took her to the Country Club, filled her with booze; then for whatever reason, possibly sound, they dumped her in my local, jetlagged and demoralized. The regulars, or a group of them, gleefully carried on the process of destruction; she faces them, tearstained and defiant. They want her dead, she knows that now. Very well, she will grant their wish. She will kill herself; then they will be happy.

I wasn't going to come in at all; for several reasons, but largely to do with those same regulars, I had decided to give the place a miss for a month or so, maybe for keeps.

Jane decided otherwise. She's a bright, vivacious girl who has probably forgotten more about horses than most folk ever knew; with her friend, she runs a livery stable a mile or so from town. I opened my mouth to protest, but it was already too late. My arm had been gripped, in no uncertain manner: it seemed my presence was required. At least, she deemed it necessary.

Death threats are not things to be dismissed too lightly. I'm fairly certain it's the gin that's talking; but can one ever be wholly sure? Steinbeck has a chilling little scene in which a depressive is mocked; people who threaten that sort of thing never carry it through. His character recognizes the truth behind the jibe, and sorrowfully drives an icepick into his heart.

The Swedes are tender about their allegedly gloomy nature. As well they might be; it's part of the popular image that has been foisted on them. Not long back though, a Swedish acquaintance took his jacket off and showed me the scars of his second death attempt. The sight was chilling; it was as if he had pressed both arms wrist to elbow on a bacon slicer. His first try had been by hanging; but like Roger Mason in Golding's classic book, the stress factor let him down. With him, it was to be a case of third time lucky.

I'm well aware all is not sweetness and light. My friend's father, an amiable, gravel-throated man, has told me the odd time to take care never to have a daughter; her disputations with him are spirited to say the least, while if the subject of World War Two crops up it's best to stand back from the line of fire. He knows his country was neutral; she knows trains for the concentration camps were allowed to run through. Tom, the RAF man, always emptied the Elsan over Stockholm; he'd lost friends to the accurate anti-aircraft fire. But right now that's all beside the point. This girl is in trouble; and metaphorically, the knife is being twisted. Her friend thought I could help; but how is a very good question.

She told me once she couldn't remember how many times she had been Lucia Queen; the ancient, magic creature who walks on the shortest day, to call back the light. She said once she would walk for me; bring the spiced drink, the little cakes of midwinter. She still has her costume; the white dress with its scarlet belt, the glowing diadem. She never got round to it, which was probably just as well. England being what it is, or rather what it has become, she would probably have been run in for disturbing the peace; in any case where would she have got her train of attendants, the Star Boys and all the rest? These things are best done properly, or not at all.

She has renewed her promise of extinction. I take her wrists, shake to make her attend.

"It is not permitted. You do not have the right."

She stares at me dazedly. Her body is her own. It is hers to dispose of if she chooses.

"It is not. You are Lucia Queen. You are the Lightbringer. If you die, the sun will not return. The world will be dark."

Well, well. Maybe I missed another vocation; I should have got a job writing scripts for Ingmar Bergman. But necessity, as is well known, works wonders for the thought processes.

Something registers with her. Impossible to say what; but her mental tack changes abruptly. She stands up uncertainly, points a wavering finger at her tormentors.

"There. You hear. So I do not care what you say. I do not care what any of you say. Why don't you all—beep—off?"

To my amazement, it's exactly what they do. They have been watching the charade with a species of fascination; they look at each other, open their mouths, and close them. The whole group files out silently.

Maybe though it's not all that surprising. They are good at pulling things to pieces, these denizens of Waitrose-on-Thames; reassembly though is a little outside their skill. All the King's horses and all the King's men couldn't put Humpty together again. Not at least if the threat had been carried out.

It takes another half hour to calm their one-time victim down sufficiently to pile her into her friend's battered Minor. The job accomplished, Jane takes a deep breath, releases it slowly. "Thanks a lot."

"I didn't do a sight. Will she be OK?"

She peers into the car. But it seems nature has taken over; Lucia Queen has crashed out, conclusively. She nods. "She'll be fine."

"As long as you're sure." I take a breath myself. "We shall have to have dinner sometime."

She considers. "Yes. I'd like that. 'Bye." She eases away from the kerb, heads off into the night.

So it's easy for me. All the father-figure stuff. If that's how folk care to think of it. I suppose in a way it was; that time at least. I knew the Queen though; her little friends merely committed *lèse-majesté*. If anybody was left with egg on their faces it was them, not me.

Jane is an interesting lass. We talked once about Mary Stewart's output of romantic thrillers. Not surprisingly, *The Airs Above the Ground* particularly intrigued her. In the book, the old Lippizaner reveals its origins by going into its routine to the strains of a distant circus band.

"That's something I've wondered about ever since I read it. Is it possible? The horse remembering like that, after all those years?"

She sips her drink. "I don't see why not. Horses aren't stupid; some of their owners perhaps, but that's another thing." She mentions another writer. His name is very much a household word. "I used to like him too."

"Why don't you now?"

She purses her lips. "He made a bad mistake in one of his books. It really got to me. I know it's stupid; I mean, he's not a vet. It put me right off though. I don't read him now; I keep wondering about the rest."

It's a new angle on the paranoia bit. The thought of somebody throwing your book at the wall is always unsettling. Even if you're never going to meet them; but there's more involved than personal discomfiture. A hallowed convention is at stake; the suspension of disbelief, no less. How that squares with punk-gobbledegook I have no idea; but frankly I don't much care.

There's more to it than that of course. In a story I wrote that I called "The Shack at Great Cross Halt," the American girl (she wasn't American at all, but I was trying to be too subtle) makes the point to the "Rural" she has saved. "It's like everything we do, every little thing, all gets itself wrote down somewhere. First to last, right through. Don't matter none, ain't nobody goin' to do anythin' about it. Ain't nobody there *to* do anythin'. But it's all there, just the same. It'll still be there, come the next million years. Even though it don't matter...." Positively Buddhistic; we're back to the empty mirror. There is a certain charm though in the notion of irrelevance. God stops being a schoolmaster, ebony ruler poised to to rap our knuckles; but that would be no comfort to certain of the English. Or to our masters; the *serein* would start again.

Which might seem comfortably iconoclastic. I only wish I could be that simple-minded. Opposing the Establishment, rejecting the idea of God, may well have an appeal for the very young; but the viewpoint is altogether too narrow. When I first moved to Salisbury, an earnestly religious friend asked if the sight of the Cathedral would offend me. It wasn't the first time her blinkered outlook had taken me aback. Not long before, she had been affronted at the buffoonery that took place in the Close, at the end of a city festival; it didn't seem to her to show a proper respect. Though her own relationship with her Lord seemed scarcely less basic. "It's like a marriage," she proclaimed once dreamily, "in which one partner is perfect...." I hauled my jaw shut, with a certain amount of effort. The Ecstasy of Saint Theresa is not uncommonly ascribed to a cause more earthy than religious fervor; but this was positively anthropomorphic. Once more, all one could really do was tiptoe quietly away. Or leave Betjeman to answer. Amid his calculated woffling, he came out with some startling shafts. The Business Women crouch in their frail bed-sitters; God flashes from the eyes of a well-dressed tart. Who knows, maybe I even caught the odd glimpse myself; in Lemady, and my distraught Lucia Queen.

One definition of Romanticism is the predominance of content over structure; but the idea can't be cut and dried as easily as that. Or so neatly pigeonholed. J.S.B. can be shattering; and he was formal enough for most. Beethoven came unstuck the opposite way. The young girl taking his shoulders, turning him to see the raving of the audience after the first performance of the *Ninth*, is the very stuff of romance; but her noble family reminded him soon enough of the structure of society. The brimming chamber pots left scattered round his lodgings, the ear trumpets stained with pus, are reminders of another sort. Maybe it's best to settle for just having a romantic streak.

I'm sitting cross-legged on the floor of my favorite Indian restaurant. On this night of nights, the musicians have disposed themselves on the carpet in front of the bar; if I wished to speak with them it seemed proper to join them. The sitar player touches the complex instrument on her lap, with its banks of shimmer-strings; they resonate in sympathy as the chords are touched, to impart the haunting, graceful sound. She smiles. "You like my music?"

My word, I must have supped not wisely but too well. "Madam, your music is almost as beautiful as you are."

Well. At least she won't crown me with the sitar; those things come expensive.

She doesn't crown me at all. The smile broadens, becomes flashing. The compliment is accepted in the spirit in which it is intended, to my immense relief.

I ask if the players would like a drink. Again, I am uncertain as to the response; but the matter is rapidly resolved. It is most kind; they will have large brandys. The restaurant owner serves them, smiling. He is more than usually resplendent. To mark the occasion he is sporting his most dazzling cummerbund; for this is New Year's Eve.

I owe my presence to an inspiration on my colleague's part. We saw the posters in the windows a couple of days before. If it wasn't too late, he would like to bring his family. Seeing the year out Indian-style would be a new experience; would I like to join them?

We were lucky; a single table remained. But he tends to be fortunate in that sort of thing. He once closed up the bookings for the Covent Garden Ring cycle in the middle of a raging thunderstorm. The passers-by had dived for shelter; Floral Street was scattered with the robes of *Boris Godunov*. But that, as they say, is another story.

I go back to our table. The drummer comes across to us. He is a diminutive, beaming man, wearing a vivid spotted shirt. I have a question for him. His playing is superb of course; but there's an extra quality. Something beyond the sound of India, something I can't place.

His grin threatens to become terminal. He was born in Bombay; but he grew up in East Africa.

Of course. Fanshawe's great *Sanctus*; the so-called musical travelogue that has haunted me for years. It's obvious enough once it has been spelled out; there's a quality to the cadences that is somehow wholly African. After that he sticks his thumb up to us each time before breaking into one of his extraordinary riffs. He climaxes his performance in a fitting fashion. It's my first and only chance to hear *Auld Lang Syne* to tabla accompaniment.

On the way back to the car we pass a pub well known to me. The denizens are still going strong; raucous voices are overlaid with the crashing of glass. I realize what the phrase "culture shock" can mean. Walking into that roomful of saris was like walking into a nest of butterflies; but I'm back to reality. This is Waitrose-on-Thames.

My colleague takes me to Brick Lane. The shock is repeated. All I knew it from was the reporting of the National Front riots; endless shots of residents sweeping up broken glass. I was left with the distinct though unspoken impression that it was a dubious area, best done away with. The reality is something else. The blaze of light from it shows above the roofs of derelict warehouses; it's like a street decked endlessly for Christmas. In the Lane itself, restaurants vie one against the next. There are supermarkets, delicatessens, dress shops. Wedding saris glitter; the embroidery, I know, is done with thread of gold. In one place we even come across a vending machine, placed boldly in the doorway of a closed shop. I haven't seen such a thing for years; the new breed of English yobs would dispose of it in minutes. It's dispensing curry-flavored chewing gum; a Cellotaped notice bears a warning to passers-by. CAUTION, it proclaims. VINDALOO; VERY HOT.

Before, I'd been in two minds about the Front; after all everybody has a right to a point of view, distasteful though it might be. Now I see just what they were trying to destroy. Something they couldn't build for themselves; or put back together once they had broken it apart. It's the social equivalent of a piano-smashing contest. At least it's good to make one's mind up for once, see things in simple terms. That's the trouble with romanticism though, always has been; before you know where you are it's turned political, and you've taken up a stance. I planned a novel round the idea once; but for a variety of reasons it never got itself done.

I write a story I call "The Ministry of Children." The heroine, a sadly-harassed schoolgirl, finds herself the focus of a siege. She asks for the Minister himself to attend. The baffled Head asks what will happen if he doesn't. Her answer has a certain disastrous simplicity. *"Then I'll say how he broke his word....'"*
I found it refreshing to work with young characters. They can often be wrongheaded; but their viewpoint has a directness and simplicity. The doomed Signaller in *Pavane* was one of the first. I used the device a number of times later; so much so that they were finally nicknamed Apprentice Stories. Which was fair enough.

When the character concerned is female, another suspicion materializes at once. In a little London club—there's no Kummel on the handle of the door, but Betjeman would have loved it—I am engaged in conversation by a smallish, amiable-looking man. He much enjoyed my novel *Kiteworld*. Well, that's very gratifying. He particularly admired my handling of the little orphan girl, Velvet. Even more satisfying of course.

He is removed, adroitly, by friends. They tell me later the tack he would certainly have taken. He's always disarming at first; he makes a speciality of it. In fact the alarm bells had already sounded, though I was no less obliged for the intervention. It saved me having to suggest that he go away. Some so-called fans get the knife out on the second meeting; his was already honed. Common as it is, it's a mental attitude I've never really understood. All writers guard against it in their various ways; for the most part, my defense took the form of simply not being around.

For writers, I suppose one might say all performers. In his jazz-playing days, my colleague made a point of never accepting drinks.

If pressed, he would settle for a bar of chocolate. The putdown was never understood; that requires a modicum of wit.

I suppose the love/hate response reached a peak with the death in a car smash of the actor James Dean. A black market in police pictures of his mangled corpse was widely reported, though in Dean's case matters were obviously complicated by a variety of sexual hangups. Much of the rest can probably be simply explained by jealousy; the jealousy of no-hopers for the successful, or those assumed to be successful. If of course jealousy can be classed as a simple emotion. Asked by an interviewer about what he styled the pressures of success, David Frost, as he was then, made a faintly chilling answer. He agreed they existed; but how did they compare to the pressures of failure?

Liking for female characters must obviously mask some deep hangup. The allegation never bothered me overmuch. It wasn't worth answering; leastways, not when I considered the tacky, self-revealing mess others could achieve. An internationally-fêted writer of thrillers, who in other respects was perfectly competent, always embarrassed me when he got to the naughty bits; I said more than once I was convinced he died a virgin. My childhood idol Richard Jefferies, in other respects a faultless describer of the English scene, spoiled his output with prurience whenever a woman hove in sight; and there have been many more. Their women aren't women at all; they're *Sex-Puppen*. The phrase tends rather to slip out; but my agent, a thoughtful and hard-working German, agrees at once. He knows about that sort of thing though; he's been through the odd hoop himself.

Sex fetishism often shows clearest when a male writer adopts, or tries to adopt, a female psyche. Even Wyndham, in other respects a technician of great skill, couldn't wholly avoid that particular trap. A woman editor, who is also a novelist in her own right, sums it up adroitly. "I know what you mean. You get things like, 'I walked down the street, my long dress swishing,' instead of, 'I went shopping.'" Faced with the problem myself, I decided on a relatively simple answer. I'd put what I've seen called the POV (point of view, I presume) out of my mind altogether and just tell the story. In my book *The Inner Wheel*, Libby Maynard details her life as far as possible as one of my male characters would. It had to be like that; or I'd have been back with the earth-tides and all the rest before either she or I could turn round and scratch. It seemed to work moderately well, though it isn't a device I would choose to repeat. A bit like Ravel, after penning his deceptively simple *Boléro*. It's said he remarked to a friend that he felt he had got away with it once, he wouldn't chance his luck again.

While talking at Cambridge, the subject of Libby unexpectedly crops up. I explain to the questioner how I approached the job; but he's not completely satisfied. He takes the point readily enough; but leaving it aside, there's still a residual feeling that the thing was written by a woman. Which is interesting to hear of course. Maybe I harbor multiple personalities; I've been taken over, as the mysterious Fiona Macleod seemed to take over the author William Sharp. I wouldn't think so though; it's pretty dubious psychology. Anyway, while Libby became real enough she always remained satisfyingly external.

Walking in London, a friend observes that I'm a bit of a fraud; he seems to know the city much better than I do. Obviously he has the promotion of *Kaeti & Company* in mind. The answer is equally patent. If he chooses to believe cover blurbs, it's his lookout not mine.

Actually, knowledge of the city was a useful hook from which to hang the copy. At least it made the point that the location was not rural. Though while working on the proposals I exercised a fair degree of caution. To be strictly accurate, "knowledge of its highways and byways" should have read "some of its byways," and those mainly by courtesy of my colleague's encyclopedic storehouse of facts. After all, who else but he would know the nickname of the roughest pub in Walthamstow; or dart aside to show me one of the last streetlamps in the city still running on sewer gas? It's always an error though to qualify promotion copy. What you've got just has to be the greatest; if even you have doubts, who else is going to take you seriously?

I used the same care when writing my alleged review, for much the same reason. When *The Chalk Giants* appeared, some pundit or other described the writing as "swaggeringly stylish." With the unerring nose of such people for the anti-sell, the publisher's promotion department featured the line on the wrapper. Maybe if they'd used more than half an eye, and given it more than a split second of their attention, it would have been different. *Sorry, parents.*

Use of female characters was another handy peg; I employed it in most of my own promotion for Kerosina, though I was pleased enough to lose it later on. Strictly speaking, the preference is more apparent than real. I admit to a soft spot for Kaeti, in common, I discovered, with quite a few more; certainly I wrote more about her than anybody else, but if people are counting, and it seems a fair few do, then Sergius, the sad Romano-Celt from *The Boat of Fate*, was my longest continuous effort, while a lot of my stuff was conspicuously male-oriented. *Kiteworld* in particular; I was delighted when Rand and the Mariner hit it off so well, and I realized they were going to add a key section to the story. There wasn't exactly a feeling of relaxing; writing is never that easy, or shouldn't be. But I felt I knew more surely where I stood.

The Mariner from *Kiteworld* was a character I felt very happy working with. Like most, he was based on a real person; for the record, I'll just call him Jim. He was a well-built, pleasant-faced young man who sported a luxuriant moustache. Many times I saw him turn girls' heads in the street, something of which he seemed genuinely unaware. I had known him a couple of years, and knew something of his history. He was an engineer, and had served his time on oil tankers; till his wife, a pretty, fair-haired northerner, tired of the wandering life and insisted on coming ashore. Now, he worked on the mainframes of computers; for relaxation, he drove a massive Honda 900. He asked me casually one day if I'd like a spin; but I shook my head. "Can't, I'm afraid; haven't got a helmet...."

He was back a day or so later, with a spare helmet clipped to the machine's frame. I gulped, and considered taking to my heels. The Centaur symbolism had never appealed, even in the balmy days of my youth; in fact I'd never been aboard a real bike at all. Just the odd scooter; and they had been hair-raising enough. Though as Jim later explained, they were actually far more dangerous machines. However, I was fairly caught. I climbed on; later, whispering along at sixty and chatting over the sound of the beautifully tuned engine, I found the experience curiously agreeable. And there was a compensation. Marching into a favored local, in which my antipathy to two-wheeled transport was well enough known, I indicated the bench that ran along below the window of the public bar. "Crash helmets there, Jim," I announced in lordly fashion. "Rule of the house...." It's not often one sees a person's jaw actually sag; satisfyingly, the landlady's chin all but hit her chest.

Later in the year—on Christmas afternoon, to be precise—Jim unexpectedly appeared. He and his wife were splitting up, he told me. The move ashore had been a mistake; at least, it hadn't led to the reconciliation he had hoped for. He was going back to sea.

I was a little torn. One doesn't encourage the loss of licences; on the other hand, there seemed more important things at stake. I poured him a whisky, then another. By degrees, he talked himself into a better mood; agreed maybe it wasn't the end of the world, there was always another chance. They started a family a short time later; but after that I lost touch with him. He went back to Australia, where he had in fact been born. England, he had decided, was no place to bring up kids; and I've seen little since to make me think him wrong.

Before he left, he repaired a typer for me; very ably too. Asked what he wanted for his trouble, he was terse. "A story...." The story was "Kitemariner." When I asked what he thought about it, he was equally firm. "It's OK. It's about Karen and me in a way; but there's a lot like us. We're not unique...."

Neither am I of course. Far from it. I certainly wouldn't claim I saved his marriage. Maybe he hadn't intended to split at all, he just wanted a sounding board. But if I helped at all, that's fine by me.

One other memory of Jim stands out sharply. On impulse, we drive down to Bristol to see the *Great Britain*, then at an early stage of her restoration. Clad in compleat steel this time; he takes his car. Naturally, I couldn't want for a more knowledgeable companion. Save in one respect. We walk round her finally, stand at the bow staring down into the great dry dock; the dock in which she was built, and that she fits to the inch. "What the hell," he says, "is wrong with that hull? I never saw lines like that...."

Realization dawns sharply. Above the waterline she's bluff-bowed; the tumble-home of her sides echoes the ships of an earlier age. Below water she's a clipper, sleek and fast. It's a new insight on Brunel's unique genius; the lengths to which he had to go to appease the traditionalists, placate the nervous.

"Damn me," says Jim. "You're right. The crafty old sod...."

We drive up to the great suspension bridge. We've both seen it from a distance, but never stood on it. We pay our toll as foot passengers, walk to the centre, stand and feel the whole structure thrill like a live thing at the passage of each car. He stares down at the wrinkled, immensely distant river, up to the traceries of supports. "I don't want to worry you," he says after a time. "but speaking as an engineer, I don't *think* those things are strong enough."

Good on yer, mate. Good luck, wherever you might be.

To my faint amusement, a certain horror was expressed when I put up my own blurbs for *Kaeti & Company*. The operations of the Kerosina crew in other respects wouldn't bear too close a scrutiny; nonetheless it seemed highly improper to them for an author to furnish his own promotion material. For my part I had a lively horror of amateurs getting their hands on the job, particularly in a corporate capacity. I understand the Chinese national anthem was composed by a committee; if all the verses are sung it takes about twenty minutes to get through it. In any case, there was an undeniable advantage. As I pointed out, I already knew what the damned book was about; so I wouldn't have to waste time reading it again.

Not strictly true of course. It seemed important to establish some sort of overview; I spent a long time poring over the text, attempting to evaluate it. The factor I had made a hardnosed joke about worked to my disadvantage; objectivity was that much harder to achieve. If I managed it at all. I'd like to think I did; after all, twenty years of slogging away in advertising just had to count for something.

It wasn't in fact the first time I had done such a thing. I offered my own blurbs for my collection *Ladies from Hell*; but those were aimed at the waste bin, on the principle that if the production department didn't have something to throw out they wouldn't be seen to be doing their job. They obliged, substituting the usual pallid, revealing thumbnails. Among other things, I had taken the opportunity to explain and develop the title idea; but of course authors don't know anything about copywriting either.

I took the same view with each of the titles I produced for myself. The writing part was over; they had become commodities, to be packaged and promoted like any others. Again, a psychologist might find such a positive and complete changing of hats at least a little interesting. I would call it professionalism; but there may well be other interpretations.

The process by which characters sometimes appear to take over their own destiny is an interesting one. It's often described in those optimistic pamphlets on how to write best-sellers, that seem to be produced in a fairly steady stream. Various phrases are used; a story "catching fire" is a favorite, though I would feel if the typer threatened combustion it would be high time to go out and have a beer. Something of the sort can happen though. The intervention may be quite explosive; so much so that it is again tempting to credit an external source; as ever, the trick is to prove the contrary. In my piece "Missa Privata," the young soprano turns on the commissar-like character who has appeared to inform her that her career is over with savage gutter language. It took me aback, till I realized how right it was; it's a true reflection of her inner torment. The act of contrition and sacrifice is complete; the father she had loved so dearly is dead. In the manner of the bereaved the world over, she will fling herself into oblivion with him.

Quite often real events will coincide with the construction of a story in such a way as to reinforce the notion of an external agency; startlingly so at times. While I was planning "Missa" my colleague, enlivened as ever by the prospect of a London setting, undertook to drive me from the crematorium where the piece opens to the Albert Hall. It was to simulate Stella's return, with her Korean pianist. I was obviously hypersensitized by the recent death of my own father; it seemed to me, sitting in the unexpectedly lovely grounds at the start of the trip, that a daisy grew for each burned soul that had received no plaque. Though Peter later deliberately broke the mood. Parking in Prince Albert Street, he remarked cheerfully that it had been a new experience; it was the first time he had gone to Golder's Green and come back with the same number in the car. During the drive, the absence/presence of Stella in the back seat had become almost oppressive; I'd like to think she smiled too, albeit wanly. Only a few days later, we were driving in a deserted part of Town when an old wino appeared. Something about the car enraged him; he seized a heavy wooden traffic sign, raised it above his head and charged. Ever quick-witted, my colleague shot the lights; there was nothing to be gained by arguing, save a dent in the door. The weird little episode provided a parallel incident in the story.

In the nature of things, the Lady Kerosina grabbed a lot of limelight from the male protagonists of *Kiteworld*. I was uncertain what the Reverend Lewis would make of her, for reasons far removed from the usual childish concerns over the opinions of vicars; but she was certainly one of the book's more bizarre characters. In the event, he dismissed her fairly briskly; he said he was sorry for her, and had found her a little pathetic. I doubted the adjective would apply if one found oneself on the wrong side of her favor; but it was close enough to what I had felt myself for me to be well satisfied. She's certainly sad, and in the long term she has to be a loser. At the start I planned an archvillainess, but I found I couldn't carry through. *Sex Puppen* are exactly that; inflated dolls, with no insides at all. Rather I saw Kerosina in a Dorset field, crying with rage because she forgot the tent-pegs.

Romanticism strikes at unexpected moments. I stare at the famous house brick, hanging in midair. Virtually any gas can be induced to lase; sodium vapor imparts exactly the right orange-yellow tone. I don't try to touch the thing because I know my hand will pass through. Neither do I peer behind the holographic plate, as a baby will crawl behind a television set to find the dog that has just run out of frame; though it seems there are enough doing exactly that. Later, in the undercroft of the new Coventry Cathedral, a slimly-drawn cross bars my way. It moves as I move, challengingly; and *The Last Ballad of True Thomas* returns with increased force. "*I ha' harpit a shadow out o' the sun, to stand before your face and cry....*" I wonder what Kipling's vivid, restless imagination would have made of it. "The Light Fantastic," they called that first holographic exhibition. Not far from the mark; and a damned good copy line too. Even the circuitry was startling; the glowing, impossibly straight threads of color, traversing the walls between lasers and exhibits. But human nature soon rears its ugly head. This will work wonders for the porn trade; like the video revolution did in its day. I saw the initial BBC transmission; the hands of the studio clock jumping back impossibly, two hours in time. The first spools were like cartwheels, inches across; till some bright spark tried angling the record and playback heads. Snuff movies and the rest weren't thought of then; but they weren't far away.

Lasers are a fine tool for science-fictioneers of course. Not that junk about incidence and reference beams though; that's boring old textbook stuff. The need is to be creative, get the old Sense of Wonder going. So how would it be if the pilot—female of course, it's always more telling if they're women—if the space ship pilot uses a laser to cut her own legs off, solve the weight problem that way? Then the child who has stowed away can stay on board. It's a new twist; provides a happy ending too, of sorts.

I have news for anyone remotely interested. The porn is already with us; like other things, it starts between the ears.

A hedge of light springs up round the great spire of the Cathedral. The beams twitch inwards, converge on the cross at its tip. It hangs against the night sky, silver and unreal. "Laser light," the local pundits explained knowingly, watching the rehearsals; later, the press copied. I didn't bother to point out the tautology. The way it's catching on, the BBC will be picking up on it soon; maybe already have. It will be acceptable then; it will have received its hallmark of respectability.

The source may well be lasers, optically diffused; but I shouldn't think so. Pencil spots would serve the purpose just as well. Either way, I wonder what the old men would have thought; the men who floated the tallest building on earth on a four-foot raft of brushwood. Its integrity was doubtful; till Golding's Dean Jocelyn pinned it to the sky with a Nail from the True Cross. Would it have survived, if the relic had not been there? We shall never know; because the matter was not put to the test. It's another of the Gotama's Unanswerable Questions. In *A Case of Conscience*, Father Ruiz-Sanchez begins the ritual of excommunication as a process for the large scale processing of lithium reaches its critical point, and the distant planet on the television screen obligingly blanks out. "Logic may have circular propensities," explains the Master in *Kiteworld*. "Or approach the condition of a sphere; the ultimate, incompressible form." The Sense of Wonder pervades the Blish novel, no less than Golding's masterpiece; but in that form it has little wide appeal. A certain *cachet* is missing. Sexual disfigurement perhaps; something the readers can relate to more directly.

It's not so much that we live in harsh times; though the claim is made increasingly, it seems with a species of pride. Uncomprehending would be a better term. "That's the trouble with emotions," says the proto-Maggie in my book *The Chalk Giants*. "They miss what they can do, and make a lot of noise about what they can't." Kaeti's adventures are uncompromising enough in places; but the harshness is of a different order. In the introduction to her first story, I suggested those lusting after blood should get themselves off to a casualty unit, or watch a Caesarian section. Then, surely, they would be satisfied; if they didn't pass out on the spot.

I ask a writer who has made a name for a certain type of quasi-Celtic fantasy how he squares the vista of lopped-off heads and hands with his much-publicized pacific nature. He has his answer ready. "It's easy. None of it's real; they're cardboard characters, bleeding red ink." At an extramural session run by London University I make the same comment to an audience member who has been becoming increasingly vociferous about certain alleged brutalities in my own work; but she rises in her wrath. It's not like that, it's not. The things I describe always seem so real. They leave her chilled. "I'm sorry. I told you I try to make it all phoney. If I fail, it's a cross I have to bear. They call it good writing...." It shuts her up. Leastways, she leaves to catch a bus; which I suppose comes to the same thing, in practical terms at least.

At a writers' workshop in Glasgow I'm presented with a gruesome little morsel. Amid the welter of arbitrary carnage, one phrase stands out particularly; a victim is described as "hosepiping blood." Piercing the aorta might produce such an effect briefly, though it chills me to think about it. I ask if anyone in the room has seen such a thing; if there is anyone present with medical or first aid experience. The would-be authors seem baffled, and a little annoyed. What has that to do with the story? I realize I've hit the old snag. Writing has no connection with reality; they are just words. It's what the cosy aniline blind is for. Let's jump into the ghetto, folks, and pull the ghetto in after us. The red ink can spurt then, to its heart's content.

There is of course no reason why a writer should shackle his or her imagination. True enough; but again a misconception is involved. Or merely shallow thinking. In an early song cycle, Britten set the words of the so-called Surrealist poet Rimbaud. But Rimbaud was a very young man, who achieved a brief literary lionhood and vanished. The form could not be sustained; truly abstract writing is as hard to achieve as "abstract" art. The Green Knight is weird enough in all conscience; but faced with the tempting of his powerful consort, Gawain's ducking and weaving has an earthy realism that gives the poem much of its force. A young shop assistant admitted cheerfully he couldn't read my "Anita" stories; they were "too tough" somehow, despite the overlay of whimsy. While in *Pavane*, the Provost Marshal's nail is damaged by a passing pistol ball. It made certain reviewers wince. We don't react to the notion of a shattered body, fountaining blood or whatever. The image has no meaning for us; it's comfortably gross. We all know what it's like though to tap our finger with a hammer; it stings, which is what the passage was designed to do.

Kaeti didn't really have a birth; rather, she materialized from the dark, much as I suggested in my little introduction. Many girls and women contributed to her psyche. It didn't seem to lessen her appeal.

Planning her first story, I knew little about her except that she came from London. And that she was from the wrong side of the tracks. It was a little quirk of mine; a glottal stop had always been guaranteed to stop me in my tracks. As long as it was originated by a pretty girl of course. My colleague saw it happen to me once in the

Strand. He is not a man given to displays of emotion; but on that occasion he positively guffawed.

The curious little trick of speech, shared notably by Londoners and lowland Scots, is not what it might appear at first. As students of accents are fond of pointing out, it by no means indicates laziness of diction. If anything, the reverse is true; the checking of the breath disrupts the smooth flow of consonants and vowels, calls for extra effort. There indeed might be a clue to its essential nature. Used excessively, the device verges on the truculent; its exponent is challenging the world, throwing down a gauntlet to the socially superior, or those deemed to be such. The protest is obvious; though as in all things, excess signals weakness rather than the reverse.

If Kaeti didn't have a birth, she had a very definite christening. I knew what I wanted to do, in the first piece I wrote about her; stand the vampire legend on its head, for starters. Or rather the celluloid, increasingly seedy myth that had grown up round Bram Stoker's relatively blameless book. It had been done before of course, everything has. I had come across the odd example; but they had seemed thin. The National Health Service providing the necessary diet of blood, and so on. It was an insult to everybody and everything in sight; not least the NHS.

The girl protagonist had already appeared; but I still lacked a name, and name magic, as ever, was a potent force. I flicked idly through the *Radio Times*; there happened to be a copy on the drawing board. I saw *The Blue Max* was to be shown later in the week. I made a note of it. A fine movie, finely photographed and played; I hadn't seen it since its outing on the big screen, it would be well worth watching again. I glanced down the cast list. I had forgotten the film name of the beautiful but brainless woman who proves Stackel's undoing; I saw it was the Countess Kaeti.

It wasn't possible. A girl with an East End father, bearing an old, poetic German name? Somehow though, it suited; it had just the right ring of faint improbability. Further, it hinted at the other half of an unusual family tree. And more ramifications; the Elsan being tipped out over Sweden, all the rest. Kaeti though wouldn't necessarily be aware of them. Nor would she need to be; Jewish and Scandinavian was a mettlesome mixture in its own right, without adding complications.

Kaeti rapidly acquired a brace of godfathers; but then, she didn't seem to be a girl to do things by halves. One was my colleague; as ever, the mention of London was enough to engage his attention. The other was my friend George. At one time he ran a fruit and veg stall in the Roman Road; by his own claim, he was a graduate of the Bethnal Green School of Martial Arts and Flower Arranging. An East End girl couldn't want a better mentor. When the book finally appeared he showed his appreciation in a way unique to him, by solemnly declaring me an honorary Londoner. It made me a little thoughtful. I had been ordered once, peremptorily, never to write about the city again as I would never understand it. I hadn't been too impressed at the time; the giver of the fiat lived a mile or so from Marble Arch, and would complain extensively whenever forced, as he put it, to go to Town. I was surprised to hear he had become a pundit. Nonetheless, a certain sourness had been expunged; I felt Kaeti and I had been moderately vindicated.

There are a thousand cast-iron reasons for not attempting anything of course. Xenophobia, parochialism, what has come to be known as machismo; all will serve as an excuse. In the background, the Grey Ones lurk; or if they don't really exist, no matter. Their earthly equivalents amply fill the gap. As ever, the trick is not listening; though occasionally it comes hard. I understand elephants can physically close their ears; I've often felt it would be a useful skill to have. Mental resistance absorbs a degree of energy; and energy can always be better spent.

I was not displeased with the finished script of *Kaeti & Company*. My colleague's eagle eye picked up one slip: Borehamwood is written as one word, not two. But it was too late to correct it. I was annoyed, because as ever the aim was total accuracy; if we can't all be Shakespeare, we can at least do our homework. And a literal had slipped past me on the first page of the text. It's the classic place to find them; the brain hasn't adjusted to the discipline of proofreading, like most car accidents happening within a few minutes of getting behind the wheel. I supposed I had best become philosophical, to a degree at least. After all, I'd driven the thing up from nothing; in more ways than one. Like the Polish *Boat of Fate*, it was in existence.

The book once produced, I experience another of those mental changes of hat. The obvious way to promote it would have been with a Pearly King and Queen. Not impossible, if the launch was in London; even George could probably have been prevailed on to come along. His presence alone would have accounted for a fair few copies; I had seen examples of his charm and frenetic energy before, and he was not one to be daunted by new fields of enterprise. "What is the difference," he asked once, "what is the difference, between selling fruit and veg, and selling books?" At which my editor of the time, after a moment's thought, shook his head. "Bugger all, as far as I can see...." The venue was fixed for Glasgow though; so yet another Redskin bit the dust. "You are talking money now, my son," the Godfather pointed out, with instant pragmatism.

Initially "Kaeti's Nights," the first story, had been intended as a one-off; but by degrees the cycle gathered a momentum of its own. The turning point probably came with a pair of stories that resulted from the same trip to Town. After a visit to a publisher's offices my colleague told me the story of the block of flats that had once stood on the site; and the bomb that had crashed through, exploding in the basement as the residents took shelter. "Kaeti and the Building" was the immediate result; the tale of a young secretary haunted by a past she can't understand. Later we repaired to a favorite haunt of our own; the George in Southwark, the old coaching inn that still retains a fragment of its once-extensive galleries. The yard that had sheltered it had been demolished; the ancient building seemed to crouch in its new isolation, as the pub crouched in one of my "Anita" stories, waiting the attentions of the wreckers.

It gets to my colleague; one of the few things I've ever known that has. On the drive back though I'm curiously confident. Kaeti will put things right; it will take more than a swinging ball and chain to demolish her. And the story of the Potman was waiting to be written anyway.

Kaeti is moving now in time, if not in space; so the tale of the Sky Person, with its further image of the Blitz, seems equally a natural. I pump my colleague for his memories. After all, he lived through the experience twice; he's always reckoned bombs have a habit of following him about. His folks shipped him off to relatives in Liverpool, the day Goering transferred his attack. I try a key paragraph out on him, a little hesitantly. He's quiet for a while, seeming lost in thought; then he nods. "You know what you've done? You've written '*Guernica.*'" I blink. He's not a man to lavish praise; apart from anything else, the advertising business cures you of that. But it's still the finest compliment I ever received. If there's any credit due though, it isn't down to me. The story belongs to Kaeti, and the very particular deity who looks after such affairs; I just put it on paper.

The collection goes out the odd time before the DIY option comes along. It's bounced of course; something I'd expected, and that later on I was extremely pleased about. As usual, my agent of the time absorbs the insults. One rejection does filter back though. An "adviser," one of those curious people who haunt the fringes of the publishing scene and for the time of their tenure at least wield considerable negative clout, commits a long and involved letter. Obviously she is of the folksy persuasion; where, she asks plaintively, is the Roberts she is used to? She misses the lyricism of my early work.

Again, the chance seems too good to miss. The location is neither Dorset nor Northamptonshire; but the point would seem to have evaded her. How many high green hills are there in—beep—Southwark? You can't touch these people though, or dent their monstrous complacency. She's so glad Keith wrote; she feels she has learned so much.

She does seem to have second thoughts; if the term isn't a solecism, since there were precious few to start with. She feels a misunderstanding may have taken place, and suggests a meeting in Waitrose-on-Thames. I decline. Apart from a disinclination to pick the tab up for her country lunch, I don't feel I left much room for error. It takes a literary expert to consider otherwise.

I had often wondered how, apart from the nepotism required in virtually every walk of life, one rises to the giddy heights of advising anybody on something as complex as book production. Suddenly the answer seems much clearer. You just have to be born a Grey One.

My agent of the time, who like most agents, of the literary variety at least, has worked long and hard for not very much, is faintly disbelieving when I announce my intention to produce Kaeti as a limited edition. He asks what a thousand copies will amount to; to which the answer is automatic. "A thousand times more than—beep—all." Unfair on him, and a little waspish; but it's too late. I'd said it before I could stop myself.

The response to Kaeti is immediate, and astoundingly positive. "She's real," proclaims one woman reviewer enthusiastically. "More real than half the people you meet in the street." What's interesting is that her appeal seems to be to both sexes. "I wouldn't *want* to meet her," says a young enthusiast mournfully. "She'd hurt me by not falling in love with me...." I haven't known such general approval since the "Anita" stories were first collected; but it's obvious already I've done myself no good at all in the eyes of the trade. I said years before, in quite a different context, that an infinity of excuses can be found for most human shortcomings; but one sin will never be forgiven. Success.

The sneer I had been expecting isn't voiced; at least if it is, it doesn't get back to me. "Vanity publishing" has always been the term used for anything the trade, in its wisdom, declined. For the most part of course there's a lot of truth in it, though in my case there would have been several fairly crushing answers. In any event, it would have been technically incorrect; I carefully avoided putting a penny into the production of *Kaeti & Company* for that exact reason, though there was a fair investment of time.

The vanity merchants have been enjoying a considerable vogue lately, to which can now be added the option of so-called desk top publishing. There's a certain incestuousness involved in the notion, or can be; by pressing a variety of buttons one can massage one's own ego indefinitely, without the intervention of third parties at all. The British Library finally declines to accept such products; but their storage requirement is already expanding by a mile or so of shelving a year, and as their spokesman points out, one has to draw the line somewhere. The socialist interests set up a brief wail; but that was expected of them anyway. The trouble with ideology of any color is that beyond a certain point one's vision can only be maintained by a progressive refusal to face the facts of life.

Many years ago a young acquaintance announced grandly that he proposed to write a book. It wouldn't be about anything in particular; just odd daily thoughts. He had never shown much sign of having any, but I forbore to say so. A mutual friend was more blunt. "The Diarrhea of a Nobody," she muttered pointedly. One way and another, there's a lot of it about these days; but I suppose there always has been. Modern technology has just made it easier to produce. In William Golding's brilliant farce, *The Brass Butterfly*, a barbarian genius invents printing in Roman times. The Emperor is instantly haunted by a vision of things like the Confessions of Nefertiti's Granny. Shuddering, he makes the inventor an ambassador to China.

There are certain curious aspects to the Kaeti cycle, the foremost being the framing device, in which she and other characters are presented as players in a sort of repertory company; hence the title. By all accepted rules, it should have reduced credibility; instead it seemed to heighten it. At least it did no detectable harm, though framing mechanisms themselves are quite rightly viewed with suspicion. It's generally thought a bad idea to try and write a first novel about a character trying to write a novel; and I can quite go along with that. The opportunities for mental confusion would appear to be endless. Other rules seem made to be broken; though I would hardly expect the publishing industry, such as it is, to go along with that. Perhaps the essential word is caution; of the proper sort.

The Establishment, of course, knows what readers want; or what they ought to like. And by God, they're going to like it, if only to justify the cynicism. It's akin to the promised extinction of real ale; which is exactly what would have happened, had not CAMRA made its unlikely appearance on the scene. It's the perfect self-fulfilling prophecy; fill the pubs with the products of the continuous brewing process, and the customers either put up with it or go teetotal. If you want justification, you can always do your market research later. An editor once spelled out to me in detail how many copies of a novel he would expect to sell, how many of a short story collection and so on. I agree he was probably right; assuming you don't lift a finger. My colleague and I lifted several; we even got our whole hands in the air, just once or twice.

The phrase "gentlemanly publishing" used to be much bandied about. Certainly the grey money-grubbing that characterizes most English activities now largely precludes originality; but one wonders what if anything it replaced. An editor who had spent some time explaining in avuncular fashion how he had trained as an engineer, and had only drifted into publishing by chance, nonetheless had a query of critical importance to the text of the novel in question. At one point I had described a character tamping a pipe with his thumb. He was not a smoker, so could not be sure; but he had only ever seen the action performed with a forefinger. Would I care to comment?

I took a pipe from my pocket, demonstrated how the bowl could be filled and packed satisfactorily using the thumb, and carefully put it away again. He was satisfied; the editing stint was over. Later, having made the statutory demand that twenty thousand words be cut from my next, his MD flew into a temper when asked where in an already tightly edited manuscript the spare material could be lost. I was the author, after all; such small matters were no concern of hers. Nonetheless, she was prepared to help. If I bought a typewriter that typed twenty percent larger characters, and wrote the thing out again making sure that every page finished on the same word, I would find, ha ha, that it had been reduced by the correct amount. These things are simple you see, if you only apply your mind.

Perhaps I am lacking in humor; but I see no gentility in such nonsense. Arrogance, stupidity, crass idleness; but virtue is significant by its absence. Now, presumably, such folk have been swept away, replaced by the yuppie element. *Plus ça change, plus c'est la même chose.* Perhaps, if fiction survives in a written form at all, limited edition operations of some sort will be the final answer. I'd like to think something would be left, at least.

"Fiction" is the key word there, of course. Write an algebra primer, I was assured once, and I would have a bestseller on my hands every year for the rest of my life. But exponents of the Cinderella craft can expect no quarter. After all, it can have no significance save for the passing of time that might be better spent. "Man cannot live by bread alone" was once a comforting adage. Increasingly the West, or a major section of it, seems to be setting out to disprove it. Gandhi's famous remark about Western civilization comes inescapably to mind.

In her review for *Vector*, the critical journal of the British Science Fiction Association, Helen McNabb expanded the idea of Kaeti's reality. "It would be no surprise to be introduced to someone and be left feeling you had perhaps met Kaeti playing one of her parts...." I was never able to discuss the point with her; but I felt together we might have drawn some interesting comparisons. I had had similar experiences, and continued to have them; maybe because Kaeti herself was drawn from so many sources. Every pretty, spirited young girl I ever met forms a part of her in a way; my friends' daughter muttering sulphurous nothings about the beauty contest, and many, many more.

I'm traveling up to London on a National Coach. For some time, a lass across the aisle has been carrying on a spirited conversation with a non-committal young man. Finally, he leaves. I'm faintly surprised; I had assumed they were together. Instantly, she turns her attention to me. She's red-haired and vivacious; unlike Kaeti at first glance, but it's soon obvious who I'm talking to. She has been living in the north; now though she has come home, and her enthusiasm is infectious. She'll not leave again; leastways if she does, she'll bury herself in darkest Spain. To be in England, and not to be in London, has been a continuing pain.

The coach is taking an unusual route into the city. Unusual at least for the Oxford service. She points out the Albert Hall; I accept the information in the spirit in which it is intended. Then shop after shop she favors, pubs and discos, the hairdresser's she used to use. It's still there, after all those *months*; it seems the mere sight of it takes her breath. I smile. If I had a copy of Kaeti's book with me, I would give it to her; she could read her own life history. But I don't.

Her stop is reached finally. In the American fashion, I wish her a nice day. In response, she leaps into the air. "I've got a week," she yells. "I've got a whole *week*...." I wave, and mentally wish her God speed. Kaeti's new adventures are forming by degrees; I know already, in one of them she will use that line. After all, it's legitimate enough; I heard it from her own lips.

The Kerosina personnel assemble at the Cerne Abbas Giant. But they have their backs to the huge, sprawling figure. They are staring at the gaunt building, once a workhouse, that faces it across the road through the valley bottom. I chose it as the terminal location for my piece on capital punishment; it's where Kaeti is brought, in her guise of urban terrorist, to pay for her crimes. They're maybe surprised to find it actually exists; but then, most of what I wrote about did. As I've said, I was never too keen on the unimaginable; reality had to do instead.

For my part, I mainly feel a sense of sadness. The book is published; that after all was the purpose of my involvement. I can't help feeling it's a pity, after such a flying start, they won't go on. The writing is on the wall though; it's been there from the first. They've played Publishers; it was fun for a time, but it's beginning to sink in that somebody is going to have to do a little ongoing work. So it will be time for another game soon. Maybe they'll go back to their fantasizing; because these folk are the real dream merchants, not me. "Wouldn't it be nice to set up a publishing company sometime...." It's odd the only muscles most folk never tire of exercising are the maxillaries.

Not that there weren't moments of rarefied pleasure. The casualness with which editors, reviewers, and the like strolled up—all arse and pockets, as they'd have said in my home town—to ask if the... ah...proofs of that...er...Kaeti thing had actually arrived, was only eclipsed by the looks of blank amazement when they found out they had. "Amateurs *talk* a lot of course; but they never actually *do* anything...." Quite right; as a rule, they don't. The fly in the ointment was me. I'm not an amateur; neither is my colleague. There were hiccups of course, there always are; but a deadline is a deadline. Now the pundits will have to retrench. "Of course, they might have *started* well; but they'll never keep going...." That's going to make me grit my teeth; because they'll be right. The ambulance is going to trundle back down the hill. There's always a chance though, next time it will get stuck in a quicksand. After all, there was one in the book.

Jim Burns appears; artist extraordinary, delineator of remarkable things. Or more prosaically, the ablest airbrush technician I've come across; and I've worked with a few. Kaeti is with him. In this incarnation, her name has suffered a slight spelling change; she's Katy Courage, school friend of his eldest daughter. But the mane of hair, the vivid, long-tailed eyes, are unmistakeable.

He unwraps the four-foot slab of hardboard he is carrying. He has bobbed the model's nose slightly, in deference perhaps to previous renderings, but the hair and eyes are the same. The eyes are startling; he has caught their exact burning hazel. The Tiger snarls from the magic mohair sweater; his mouth is a red cave, opening disturbingly into Kaeti's chest. The Shadows writhe behind her; they are faceless, just as I described them, but instinct with pain. Most disturbing of all, Kaeti stares not at the viewer but past, into some Hell of her own. Considering the visual I had produced, he had observed politely that he hoped I didn't expect him to copy it. He could do better. I didn't expect him to copy; and by God, he hasn't. So it seems the truck missed the quicksand after all; the only problem that will remain is selling the edition. Always something, isn't there?

I pull into the layby, stare at the great, foreshortened figure of the Giant. Lemady stares up as well, with a sort of thoughtful intensity. She didn't know the carving at all; and I had omitted to show her a photograph. The silence continues. a minute passes; it stretches to two or three.

"We could walk up if you like. It's farther than it looks though; and it's quite steep in places."

She continues to observe the figure. "No thanks. That'll be all right."

"Well, there he is anyway. Shall we go on?"

"Yes," she says. "Yes of course, thank you." Half a mile on she speaks suddenly, with a species of awe.

"It's right up to his rib cage...."

I'm quite unable to explain why the car makes a sudden swerve; or why I laugh so much. Something to do with the clinical phrasing perhaps; but then, she wasn't a Ward Sister for nothing.

VII.

A Dorset farmer once flew a most satisfying kite. He proposed to carve the figure of Marilyn Monroe on one of the hills that face the Cerne Abbas Giant; a silhouette of the famous publicity picture, where her skirts are blowing up. The media latched onto the story; for a day or so the airwaves rang with indignation. Phrases like "national heritage" were bandied about; but the originator of the scheme was unrepentant. It was his land; also, the Giant was a sex symbol. So why not complement him with the image of a modern Goddess of his ilk?

In fact it wouldn't have worked. The figure would have been off the chalk belt; though earth carvings have not been unknown, for obvious reasons they tend to be short-lived. Nonetheless, it would have been an interesting project to work on. I would have roped out a grid and squared the job up, as I suggested in my book *The Chalk Giants.* Achieving a true right angle at the start would have been dodgy, though some simple trigonometry would undoubtedly have helped; after that the work, though labor-intensive, would have been relatively easy. The Whipsnade Lion was formed by complex surveying techniques, but they would not have been strictly necessary. Nor would such nonsense as signaling flags from the opposing slope to direct the workers, as suggested by Eric Benfield, otherwise an excellent, level-headed writer on Dorset subjects much in the style of the better-known Ralph Wightman. The fierce perspective imparted by the figure's siting would have rendered such a project impractical anyway, as a moment's thought should have revealed; but amateurs, when faced with the simplest "art" problem, always fly into a kind of quasi-mystical cloud cuckoo land, ignoring straightforward solutions, inventing difficulties where none need exist. If a professional is ill-advised enough to reveal his methods, methods as old as drawing itself, he will be deemed to have cheated in some strange way; they are "disappointed" by the obvious.

The Giant himself was formed from a grid of some sort, as his accurate proportions reveal when seen from the air, a viewpoint his constructors could never have achieved. Even his vital statistic, the one coyly never mentioned in the guide books, is not as wildly exaggerated as might at first seem.

An odd acquaintance of mine once determined to supply the missing measurement. We accordingly drove to Dorset, climbed the hill and ducked under the ropes that guard the figure, symbolically at least, from desecration. As I placed the tip of my brolly to secure the end of the tape, thunder rolled threateningly across the valley. I was faintly surprised. I hadn't realized he was a weather god as well.

A degree of irreverence would seem to be an essential part of life, though not of course in the sacred purlieus of science fiction and fantasy. But without it things can get decidedly humdrum, not to say stodgy. What is important is to be aware what one is being irreverent about. Lemady once played a record she thought hilarious. They had found Sandy's trousers, apparently, on the top of Ben Nevis; whoever Sandy was. But she also told me the legend of the Boat from Tir-na-nOg. It became, eventually, *The Boat of Fate*.

A friend tells me about the sophisticated franking machine they installed once in the Post Office Tower. Some ingenious soul discovered that if you split the postage and stuck the stamps into each corner of a letter the robot would be baffled; once inside the works, the envelopes would potentially rotate for ever. The Post Office appealed indignantly for the practice to stop; once having publicized the trick, they had no option but to remove the device altogether.

I retail the story gleefully in my favorite Amesbury bar. A customer immediately becomes indignant. People who do that sort of thing are irresponsible; they should be severely punished. The trouble is, the madder he gets the funnier he becomes; the top of his bald head flushes a deeper and deeper red. Though in a way his reaction is predictable. He organizes occasional grinding band sessions at the hotel that I have always found a pain. Nobody who perpetrates that sort of jazz could possibly understand the point. Which is of course that nobody was harmed; while the trick displayed a high degree of ingenuity. There's something in the human psyche that needs to defeat the machine, to beat the system. Thank God for it; I'm relieved to see it hasn't been wholly extinguished, despite the best efforts of our money-grubbing masters.

A couple of genial retired men own up to the great corn circle hoax. They cheerfully reveal their method, a simple enough system employing a plank and a rope. They said for fifteen years or so it had been an amusing hobby; they took sandwiches with them and a flask, and thoroughly enjoyed the mild night air. They only admitted the trick because the ever-hovering experts were about to be drafted in, and there was talk of a research grant; they didn't like to see the country's money wasted. I would have been pleased to buy them both a beer; but the mysterious pundits were naturally indignant. If they were that smart they shouldn't have been suckered in the first place of course, but more importantly they had missed out on a nice little number. Hotel accommodation paid for, the lot; with care, they could have kept things trundling on for years.

More irresponsibility, no doubt; but if the shadow of the great, tragic Norma Jean could have shown even briefly in Dorset earth, I would have deemed it no bad thing.

Lemady considers a paperback. *The Green Man*, by Henry Treece; a fine writer, quickly and gleefully forgotten by the trade. And consequently by almost everybody else. She frowns. "I don't think I really understood it. All that stuff about flying, when the Queen's talking to the little priest. Then she sends for a clean robe; why does she do that?"

"I thought it was funny. She keeps saying a Queen has to know all. She fetches him off."

"Oh...!" She flushes a spectacular deep red; I've seen if happen once or twice before. For a time I thought her seeming innocence was an act. It certainly lets her sail through situations where others would be embarrassed, or get angry. It isn't though; her mind, that is sharp enough in other matters, just fails to function along lines of innuendo. She genuinely doesn't understand.

Except maybe once. One of the tyres on the Cambridge is looking distinctly bald; she tells me she is coming into Reading, to a quick-fit place that offers good terms. When I meet her in the evening I ask if it went OK. She looks thoughtful.

"Yes, fine. There was just one thing. There was this funny man there. Got a limp, sounded as if he had a cold. He'd got some display boards with him."

"My God, that's Snuffy. Our account exec. I saw him going out of the office with them. What did he do?"

"Nothing really. There was a bit of a queue. He kept getting behind me. I tried to get out of the way; but he kept prodding me in the back with them. Everywhere I went."

I start to laugh. My revered colleague can't help being congenitally one-legged; nor I suppose is the permanent catarrh really his fault. But his foreplay certainly needs a bit of brushing up. I've had some funny ideas in my time; but prodding ladies in the back with the corners of display boards never struck me as a fruitful way of arousing passion. Of the appropriate sort at least. But each to his own.

As ever, Lemady's personality seems built of contradictions. This is the shrewd woman—"thrawn" would be her preferred word— who wouldn't let the would-be seducer see her face; and the same who when she was under training imported an electric fire into her cubicle, managed in some way to secure a connection. Other nurses copied, and the fuses blew; but she remained unrepentant. "I was freezing. It's all very well having a vocation; but that's no reason for being uncomfortable...."

There, it seems to me, is the very essence of femaleness; its ultimate pragmatism. The monks of Kyoto would understand the comment very well. A legend of the Buddha appealed to me so strongly I used it in my novel *Gráinne*, later to win what my old Latin master would have called "a pot." Asked by the great teacher who she liked best of all, a certain Queen Pasenadi answered it was herself; the Prince blessed her, and declared her wise among women. Perhaps a certain dreaminess was an essential part of her makeup too.

Just now and then Lemady's innocence and shrewdness collide, usually with impressive results. At her housewarming party, a guest admits ill-advisedly to being a psychiatrist. Instantly she is assailed by symptoms; I've seen the same thing happen to TV repairmen. The hostess joins in. For once, she isn't thinking; she's relaxing, after the sustained effort of the last few weeks. The result is predictable.

"I can't *stand* jigsaw puzzles; and I positively *scream* if somebody shows me a typewriter. What does that suggest to you?"

But the doctor, an attractive, personable young woman, has very obviously had enough. She considers for a moment before she answers.

"Inability to concentrate...."

For once, I do laugh aloud. I can't really help myself. Presumably, they used to be friends. When Lemady makes a gaffe though, she doesn't mess about; there are no half measures.

We're in a local bookshop. A display of Arthur Ransome titles catches my eye. I pick one up. *Swallows and Amazons*; I've never actually read it, though of course I've heard enough about it. I open it. "Good lord...."

The proprietress bustles up. We're not exactly the closest of friends. A week or so before, I saw a card in the window of the shop requiring an assistant to work in the back. I was a little short of ready at the time; sorting books as they arrived would have been a nice little number for a week or two. She had different ideas though. She looked me up and down, deliberately. "You?" she enunciated with horrible clarity. "God's teeth...."

So she was right; the image wouldn't really form for me either. There was no need to turn the other customers' heads though.

She peers at what I'm holding. "Ah," she says, "the Ransome. Lovely book, absolutely adorable.... Do you like it?"

"It's a rewrite of *Bevis*. Even the chapter headings are the same. 'In which they build a boat,' the lot...." Further, the blurb writer had the cheek, or the pig ignorance, to claim it's the only English novel built round a reservoir. So what happened to Coate?

The bookseller nods cosily. "I suppose there are similarities. But of course Jefferies learned a great deal from Ransome."

105

Clangers will not be dropped; they will be highly polished, and lowered gently to the ground. After all, Jefferies died in eighteen eighty-seven. I don't bother to point it out; instead, I observe the perpetrator. Interestingly, a blush starts at the roots of her hair. It spreads and richens. When it seems to have reached maximum intensity, I shake my head sadly and turn away. "God's teeth, madam. *God's teeth....*"

Lemady has watched the process with interest, though without immediate understanding. Later I comment on the bookseller's discomfort. "She went a really super color. Nearly like you."

Lemady though is indignant. Nobody, but nobody, blushes as well as her. She is in a class of her own; which is true enough.

I'm well aware someone with knowledge of hospitals and their staff might fairly remark that a mixture of innocence and brashness is a characteristic of the nursing temperament, in so far as it can be defined. So be it. Warned that Lord Alfred had feet of clay, Oscar Wilde was unperturbed. He was aware of that; but did it not make the gold more wonderful by contrast? Rebuttal or elegant evasion, the remark remains ultimately Wildean; an encapsulation of the paradox that lies behind most human relationships.

It all seems a long time ago; as the attendant said, at the Baths of Sul-Minerva. It's another world now; the Thames Valley is behind me, and a lot else besides. Except that Time is notoriously relative.

I'm sitting in the bar of my favorite hotel again. It's an elegant room, civilized and spacious; through the lounge, French windows afford a view of lawns, a wide, shallow pond. A cedar spreads elegant dark branches. It's to reach its term soon; but all States are subject to Change.

I'm chatting to a couple of girls. They materialized unexpectedly; and their appearance is very different. One is petite and formal, with the side-cropped, unmistakeable hairstyle that goes with the wearing of military caps. I've met her before; at a parade at a local Army camp, the presentation of a long service medal to a friend to celebrate, as he put it, twenty years of undetected crime. Her companion is taller by a head, jean-clad and possessed of a cascade of wild brown curls. She sips a lager, and wags her thumb disparagingly. "Wouldn't think we're sisters, would you? I can't stand her. Don't expect she thinks a sight of me either. Wouldn't know; I never really asked."

A non-committal answer would seem best. Or no answer at all. "So what do you do for a living?"

She glances at me. "I'm in domestic service." Somewhere, there's a hint of irony. "Work for this rich bloke in Hampstead. Nice little number really. I'm gettin' itchy feet though. Might go to the States; see a bit of the world."

My word. Things have changed a bit since my young days. Leastways, the image of housekeepers has; Mrs. Danvers wouldn't get a look in. I say as much, and she grins. "What about you? How do you pass your time?"

"Oh, this and that. Bit of artwork; anything that comes."

"He writes poetry," says her sister. "He sent that book to the Colonel."

"Well, it was a bit of nonsense really. How's he keeping these days?"

"About the same. Not too bad. Doesn't complain; but then of course, he wouldn't."

The hirsute Mrs. Danvers turns her nose up. "Wouldn't do for me. Bein' in the Army. All that discipline an' stuff...."

"No I don't suppose it would. Your hat wouldn't fit, for starters."

Not that her mode of transport doesn't have a certain military, or militant, air; a burly Land Rover, painted fire engine red and equipped with a pair of CB aerials that make it look as if she's about to embark on a tuna-fishing trip. I ask her if she's an enthusiastic breaker; but she shrugs. It's a laugh, or can be.

It seems most things are. Last night for instance, she rang one of those sex lines that are being pushed increasingly.

"Good lord. Why did you do that?"

She shrugs, and lights a cigarette. "To see what all the fuss was about." She blows smoke, vigorously. "Dead waste o' time though. Wanted my credit card number; kept sayin' they wouldn't do anythin' without. Must have thought I was soft. They only put tapes on anyway; it ain't the real thing." She seems to know a fair amount about the process already; for a humble Domestic at least. Somewhere, I'm quite sure Lemady is laughing. She would understand this girl; and enjoy her.

I turn down an offer of a lift home. I'm not ready to go yet; not, at least, by that vaguely uncertain route. The Land Rover charges off into the dark, its aerials whipping. A friend watches the departure sardonically. "Didn't go much on her. Right round the twist. Hands like bloody shovels anyway."

"Oh, I wouldn't say that...."

He's wrong, in fact. Right now, she's more balanced than he is; and her hands are strong and shapely. She's female, not feminine; between the words, as ever, a gulf is fixed. He can be excused though. He's got troubles of his own; right now, no women suit him. And precious few men.

I observe the little Venus of Verulam. She stands on the windowsill of my sitting room. The sill is white; the reflection from it backfills and softens the hardness of *contre jour*. You could play round with lighting all day and not get a better result. Or one more revealing of contour; which is what the whole thing is about anyway. I put the facsimile there experimentally, when it was brought by an intrigued deliveryman who was keen to see just what he had conveyed. "You'd best check it," he said. "Just to make sure it's all right...." And there she has stayed. She belongs; I couldn't place her better.

The high seat of my drawing board affords her a quiet background of grass, starred with daisies when the mower hasn't passed for a day or so. It's fitting, for this most western of images. She may well have been made on the Continent and imported; but either way, little of the Classical world remains. The pose certainly, the draperies, the Apple of Discord in her delicately modeled hand; but this girl's figure is wholly Celtic. It shows particularly in her longish, slightly flattened feet; the extremities are often not the main beauty features of the Celt.

Her right arm is extended stiffly, the hand truly a little spade-like. It's in sharp contrast with the rest of her; it hints at the first of several mysteries. Could the figure have been damaged in antiquity, and roughly repaired? An x-ray examination of the original would give a hint at least; but as far as I'm aware the experiment has not been tried.

She was made originally by the lost wax method; *cire perdue*. Eighteen hundred years later, the bronze replicas produced for the Verulamium Museum still are. The rest are cold-cast; but rubber and molten metal are not an ideal combination. One can imagine the yuppie element turning their noses up; how unprogressive these artist johnnies are! With so many undercut planes though, it's the only viable way; as ever, true ignorance is unassailable.

A major puzzle presents itself at once. Before the advent of flexible molds, copies were not practical; each figure was a one-off, perforce. The investment would have to be broken away, as we chipped painstakingly at the plaster of Paris lumps that held our treasures, back in my art school days; only to find occasionally a bubble had formed during the casting process, the figure lacked a head. These little effigies of Gods and Goddesses had a considerable vogue for a time; they were favorite features on Roman sideboards, where they presented scenes from mythology. Originally the Venus would have been the product of a little manufactory. Was the modeller able to catch that youthful freshness time and again, perhaps from a *maquette*? For youthful she certainly is; this is a girl in early puberty.

The obvious signs are there of course; the relatively unformed breasts, lack of definition round the waist and hips. Other indications are more subtle; the slightness of the calves for instance, hinting at greater fullness to come. I wonder who modeled for her; for modeled she certainly was, once on a time at least. The sculptor, the worker in clay or wax, has the same requirement as the illustrator. You can't make up the human figure; not in this detail, and with this degree of conviction. Maybe the artist prevailed on his daughter; and maybe she took a day or two to make her mind up, steel herself for the performance. She appeared then on the dais in the corner of his little workroom, blushing with a mixture of modesty and pride, the drape knotted at what Dylan Thomas called the middle of the world. There are so many possibilities; the little figure invites contemplation.

A retired Professor of Mathematics once told me a curious little joke. A millionaire decided to take up a hobby, and opted for the study of jade. So he instructed his secretary to discover the world's leading authority and book a course of lessons. This was done, and the would-be collector duly flew off in his private jet. A few days later he rang the secretary in a state of high indignation. "You reckon this guy's an expert? It's costin' me an arm and leg...."

"But what's gone wrong, sir?"

"Wrong? I'll tell you what's gone wrong. Monday, he turns up with a piece of jade. He dumps it down, and I sit starin' at it. Couple of hours later, he turns up again. 'Thank you, sir, that'll be all for today....'"

"Tuesday the same, Wednesday, Thursday; and if that ain't enough, this morning he brings a fake...."

The millionaire though was obviously a bright man; something between his ears apart from the traditional hard vacuum. When I was working with Kyril Bonfiglioli in Oxford, he once undertook just such a course of extramural classes. The subject was Aesthetics. After the last, he appeared in a stamping temper. That was positively the end; never would he waste his time on such a thing again. Like the young man in the story, I asked what had gone wrong; and he slammed down a pair of figures of the seated Buddha.

"Look at those. One's exquisite; lovely piece of work. The other's crude; backside like a rhinoceros turd. I asked *them* to tell *me* which was which; and not a peep out of the whole pack of them. After six weeks...."

But the students had waited in dismay, notebooks poised, ready to receive the words from on high. It seemed if the class had learned nothing, Bon had; and the course, as far as I know, was not repeated. By him at least.

So we know what "art" is. It's pretty things as distinct from crude; pictures stuck in frames, and hung on gallery walls. Nothing could be further from the truth. "Women in designer smocks," I said once, "modeling coy terra cotta when the mood was on them," don't qualify. Warhol's calculated excesses, Oldenburg's Soft Typewriters, and all the rest, were equally beside the point. They redirected the gnat-span attention of the glitterati for a time, if that can be claimed a virtue; but after that their purpose was complete. The whole question of aesthetics is broader, but at the same time more finely honed. Ex-

planations aren't really on though. As the great Louis Armstrong once
observed, if you've got to ask you'll never know.

Among ephemera, that straw locomotive hanging from its
Glasgow crane was much more to my taste. Its canny originator later
floated a large paper boat on the Clyde. "He's a chancer," explains a
friend. I feel I know the type. Charming, persuasive, filled with the
gift of the gab; London has its chancers too, it's a city type. Long may
he thrive; there's a sardonic quality to his constructions, their point is
in their very transience.

I stare at the mosaic pavement. The calm, strong head of
Winter watches back. The face is androgynous, neither female nor
male; a striking thing to see, appearing between little drifts of autumn
leaves. I glance at Lemady, but her face is non-committal. Maybe
she's a little spooked; it's sometimes hard to tell.

She shouldn't be. In a strange way it's as if she called the image into being, for that brief span of time. It belongs within her aura;
like the oak leaves, the strange scent of the triclinium at Chedworth,
compounded so largely of the pine logs that frame the place. These
things are Celtic; the folk Jacquetta Hawkes called restless barbarians
were drawn, instinctively it seems, toward the setting sun. And
Lemady is a Celt; it shows in her height she proclaims proudly, her
fairness, her clear blue eyes. Though they could hint at other things;
after all, she comes from the coast the Vikings harried so unceasingly.
I suggested once her preoccupation might have been misplaced; she
could have spent her time more profitably studying Old High Norse.
She was not best pleased.

The materials from which the portrait is built are simple.
Chalk, sherds; Kimmeridge shale, the poor man's jet. But as Bon was
fond of pointing out, Britain was very much the arse end of the Continent, in Roman as in later times. The materials themselves dictated the
simple treatment; but in that lies its power.

I queued half a day to see the Tutankhamen exhibition at the
British Museum. Later, a man I met casually asked me what I had
thought of it. An image popped into my mind at once.

"You know those shops they used to have on Brighton
seafront, with the brass firescreens in the windows? The sailing
galleons, and all the rest?"

He stared at me aghast. "You must be mad...."

I shrugged. I couldn't be bothered to argue. He asked, so I
answered. Gold in quantity, particularly the butter-yellow gold of the
old Egyptians, has much the appearance of brass; if looked at straightforwardly at least, without a topload of expectation. That and the
hasty, patched-together appearance of much of the tomb furniture had a
strange effect. The wooden guardian at the entrance with his formal,

110

stiffly-jutting kilt, one of the pair that originally stood at the door of the tomb, had stayed more in my mind; that and the palette of the girl Queen, still with its little smears of pigment in place. There perhaps is an aspect of aesthetics; as ever though, social awareness is not far behind. And politics tread inescapably at its heels.

The first time I came by a facsimile of the Venus I sat staring at it for most of a day; turning it, studying, enjoying the shifting play of light, the little surprises it brought. One induced a faint but definite shock. The artist's daughter had dimples on her bottom, just above the broad cleft of the buttocks. Like other dimples, they are little adhesions of the fatty layer; some women have them, others do not. This girl did; and the craftsman modeled them with care. He was someone who knew the shapes of women and young girls; and like my painter in "Our Lady of Desperation," he loved them for their splendor. Just for a moment I felt curiously close to him; the time machine we all carry between our ears had worked its charm again.

The statuette has had a chequered history. It came to light during a dig on which Barry Cunliffe worked; he was later to make his name by masterminding the excavations at Fishbourne, that revealed half at least of an entire Roman palace. A golden handshake for Cogidubnus presumably for allowing the Legions ashore unopposed, though that will almost certainly never be proved. I heard the Professor lecture once as part of one of his fund-raising tours. Lemady quite fell for him; though that was by no means unusual. She fell for one of the Navy guides on H.M.S. *Victory* once; he brightened visibly at her attention, and by degrees his talk came to be delivered more and more to her. Waspishly, I didn't tip him. He'd had his perks; and he'd still have his golden eyelashes in the morning.

They found the Venus in what had been the basement of a bronze-worker's shop; she had been thrown into a box with other fragments, to wait her turn for melting down. It was only a fire in town that saved her; during the rebuilding the cellar was filled in, and she was forgotten. She was displayed proudly in the Verulamium Museum; later, she was stolen. I wrote mournfully to the curator of the time, expressing sympathy and praising the farsightedness that had ensured, *via* the facsimiles, the figure was not wholly lost; and received a good letter in return.

There was to be an unexpected sequel to the theft. An anonymous call to the local police advised them that if they visited a common just outside the city and looked under a certain bush, they would find something of interest. And there she was, wrapped, if I remember rightly, in an old nightdress. The unknown benefactor had realized the value of what had been taken; more importantly, he or she had picked a phone up. They could so easily have thrown the Venus into a brook, or simply buried her again. As a result of a private donation the Museum

111

was equipped with a security system; today she regards the world from behind heavy armored glass. She is secure; or as secure as she can be, bearing in mind the changeable state of all things earthly. The Fact of her existence though can never be gainsaid. At the end of my novel *Gráinne*, World War Three apparently breaks out; but the vanished priestess glows brightly, as the radiation lights a holographic plate.

My first facsimile was stolen in its turn; an echo of the real event that the Museum folk found intriguing. The thief was unrepentant; at least, he put a swaggering face on things. But that is typical. Attack was always a commended form of defense; or the adding of insult to injury. Despite the harsh claims made for the late twentieth century, thieves still tend to be in a minority; perhaps they feel insecure as a result, hence the aggression. Their belligerence takes a variety of forms. I have even heard it claimed they are "strange people," and that that somehow makes them unique, and therefore of significance. In truth, their behaviour has a boring sameness. Certainly when things have been stolen from me—books, artwork, a car on one occasion, a statuette—the acts have been swathed in the same predictable *bravura*. To a large extent, I could have written the script.

The need to steal is interesting in itself. If one came across a few thousands pounds lying in a misplaced wallet, temptation would obviously be a factor; often though the value of the goods is secondary or immaterial. The drive would seem to be to prove oneself somehow smarter than or superior to the opposition, or the imagined opposition. As such, it's akin to my former employer's antics with the coin; competing for the favor of a girl who could have no real significance for either of us. Or us to her, which seemed to me more important.

The urge to appear top dog, at whatever cost in energy, also gives rise to a ploy common among the compilers of the sometimes curious ephemera known to the initiated as fanzines; the endless attempts to needle authors into a response by a variety of insults, some barbed to an extent, others merely crass. Occasionally the editors of seemingly professional mags, who one would assume to have more about them, also allow it. I was caught myself once; but that wasn't because I didn't know the game that was being played. I had just finished a long, complicated book; like Lemady I was relaxing, and my attention momentarily lapsed. It's a dangerous time; like reading the first paragraphs of a proof. Once in a quarter of a century isn't a bad record I suppose; but it's still once too often.

Occasionally the process can give rise to amusement. Quite early on, while *Pavane* was still going through its British magazine outing in fact, I did respond to an Australian "zine"; but the situation was rather different. In an outburst of juvenile spleen, a reviewer had suggested I hadn't been able to decide how one of the stories in the cycle should finish, so had supplied two endings and left it to the readers to make their own minds up. The chance of a legpull seemed too good to miss; I suggested his head be immersed in sheepdip, or whatever fluid was locally available, and went on from there. The result was predictable. First, the self-styled critic exploded into vituperation, represented as usual by a line of asterisks; second, he blamed the editor for misquoting him; third, he resigned from his high office. After that I gave the sport up. I have seen that sort of nonsense described, with apparent seriousness, as "the cut and thrust of fandom"; to me it seemed uncommonly like spearing fish in a barrel.

Again, there was a sequel; entertaining this time, and a little touching.

I received a letter from an Antipodean fan, who I learned later was elderly and bedridden; obviously he got much of his social contact from the amateur magazines. "Good on you," he proclaimed roundly. "Got the crawfishing bastard...." I was pleased to feel I had given him some amusement, however transient.

Although the thought will seem a little pompous, it can't be denied that in committing any sort of writing to print you are to an extent casting bread on the waters. A prolific writer friend once engaged in an extended correspondence with a lady in America. When she had worked through all his titles he recommended one of his pseudonyms. She wrote to say she could not understand why he had suggested such a crass and incompetent author. Later the deception somehow became known to her. It was then revealed that she was old and terminally ill, that she was a nun in a closed Order and had received a dispensation from her Mother Superior to study science fiction. In her last letter though she forgave him; she had, she said, made him her brother in Christ. The story seems more than a little suspect; but I am inclined to give it a degree at least of credence. It's really the business of the Unimaginable again. If one can imagine an event, then sooner or later it will happen; or more likely, already has.

I did once send a longish letter to a fanzine. In fact I wrote several, over a period. Some surprise was apparently expressed; my antipathy to such things seemed to be generally known, or assumed. How had the editor managed to entice me into correspondence, when so many others had failed? He asked me himself eventually; but the answer seemed too obvious to need spelling out. He had asked me, civilly enough, if I would help him build up his letter section. The magazine was well produced, obviously the product of considerable care and thought; so I was happy to help out. It's so much better though to get results the smart way, by calculated or not so calculated insult; even if it produces no response, it's more fun trying.

The tricks used by amateurs and others rapidly pall by sameness; but until one learns the rules they can be deadly. My first brush with the production side of the live action film business was almost disaster. I had been asked by a moderately well known director to write a script. It rapidly became obvious I was to be pig in the middle between him and the potential star's production company, who were picking up half the tab for my very modest retainer. Nonetheless, the situation still got to me. After a month or so of useless trekking forward and back from London, I noticed one morning my comb seemed unusually full of hair. I fingered my scalp experimentally, grabbed a tuft and tugged. It came away. I hied me at great speed to my GP of the time, a man for whom I have retained great love and respect.

"Look at this, doctor! Every time I pull my hair, it comes out!"

He observes me mildly. "I wouldn't do too much of that if I were you. You've got alopecia."

"What does that mean?"

"It means your hair is falling out. What have you been doing?"

I tell him. As ever, he is brisk. "Give it up. And rub this in. It may help, it isn't a placebo. It will probably recover by itself anyway."

He was right, it did. But the lesson was salutary; I gave up the attempt at scriptwriting the same day.

My next brush with the film and TV establishment resulted in *Molly Zero*.

The third approach was by an independent producer. Out of the goodness of his heart he was prepared to allow me to take part in his newest, greatest project. I was tired of wearing a track along the M4 though; beside which, I already had his half of the patter by heart. I wrote to say I didn't take on speculative jobs, and not surprisingly heard no more. I may of course have missed my chance of fame and fortune; but somehow I doubt it.

I often used to say I would appreciate just one con trick that hadn't been tried on me before. The BBC World Service oblige. I'm summoned to Bush House to record an interview for an arts program they are currently sending out. As usual, I'm obliging my publishers; at least they won't be able to say I'm uncooperative. In the event, I'm in and out of the place in twenty minutes. It's the fastest, most peremptory affair I've come across; if ever I saw a tape designed for the cutting room floor, that was it. I'd arranged a meeting of my own just down the road anyway, so the morning wouldn't be wholly wasted; and I built a story round the episode that covered my fare and a little beside. Nonetheless, I was advised some time later by a colleague that I should have put my expenses in to Auntie as well; there was just a chance she would have paid up. Then it would all have been profit.

An insomniac friend, who listens to the radio a good part of each night, tunes in to the program for a week or two; but as expected, the item doesn't feature. I'm frankly puzzled. Naturally my time and effort were of no account; but why bother at all with something you're not going to use?

The answer dawns belatedly. Over the producer's head will be a Series Producer, or some such title. He or she will need a constant supply of material to discard, so the egoboo can be sustained and the Corporation's salary justified. I wonder what Lord Reith would have made of it. He justified low fees, or no fees at all, by pointing out the value of the personal publicity received. Dubious of course, and unscrupulous to a degree; but what's the position when the item isn't transmitted?

Such fiascos build up a resentment; but not for the reasons that might be immediately supposed. In self defense one is forced to play the opposition's little games; or at least allow for the possibility of cheap tricks. It's demeaning; but worse than that, it consumes both time and energy. A translator friend observes that over the years more effort has gone into defeating the conniving of publishers and the like, and of course in getting paid, than ever went into doing the job itself. I feel I understand her viewpoint very well.

An editor calls to inform me a specialist bookshop has agreed to take a hundred or so signed copies of my newest. Will I come up to Town and do the necessary?

"No."

He sounds annoyed. "But it's to your benefit."

"It isn't. I've had the advance; it just means you'll go into the black quicker. Then you'll be snapping your fingers for the next. Why should I be an unpaid PR man?"

He considers. "If I pay your expenses, will you come?"

"No. Same reason. It would still be a waste of a day."

He goes silent for a few seconds. "I'll pay your expenses and buy you lunch."

"Now you're talking. We can go to the Lamb. Thursday all right?"

He still has the last laugh. But that's important, for the Image. The books finally signed, I stack them and sit back. "Well, that's that. I only hope they sell them."

He sniggers. "It doesn't matter to us if they're stuck with them. We shan't take them back. They're damaged copies now; somebody's scribbled in them all."

Of course; what was I thinking of? The outlet would have waived their sale or return clause as the price for getting my signatures. It's the oldest trick in the book; as his was the oldest line. And I still let him get away with it.

I suppose it is funny, in a way. At least it would be, if you're not the one caught in the mincer. I believe the German equivalent is something like "flesh machine." It's very apt.

The mincer has always been there of course. My ex-employer once insisted on driving me to London. I accepted with a sinking heart.

Potentially, he was a lethal chauffeur; but there was no way out. He caught me outside the station; and he never would take a gracious refusal. In Park Lane, he waved his hand expansively. "That's the Hilton, by the way."

"I know. I sold my first book on the twentieth floor. Or it might have been the twenty-first. It was pretty high up anyway."

It had been a revelatory experience. I was ill-advised enough to touch the iced water tap in the bathroom, never having used such a device. The American editor, who was moderately drunk, howled in agonized anticipation. The resultant banging and thudding took some time to fade away; I was rewarded by three or four drops of rusty-looking water. He said his secretary had apologized to him for the booking; but London was full, it just had to be the Hilton.

Not that he didn't have a certain social flair, inebriated or not. At lunch in another place (as they say), we were presented with menus in unrelieved Spanish. He threw his across the table and roared, "Flapjacks...." Flapjacks were served; and they were very good.

Later we got down to the business of books. He proudly made over the microscopic advance. He liked the thing, he announced expansively. He would be prepared to buy up to four or five like it annually. I blinked. "I should think you bloody well would...." Corny or not, *The Furies* had already taken nine months out of my life. The classic gestation in fact, as is often remarked. My agent of the time was shocked by my bluntness. I was just shocked; but the flesh machine was already hungry.

Some folk can turn the handle; and out the words come, endlessly and automatically. It's a talent I much respect; but it has always baffled me. Lionel Fanthorpe, a vicar in real life and a most urbane man, is said to hold the record for sheer numbers of books produced; while Edgar Wallace wrote novels overnight to clear his gambling debts. I have met one or two exponents of the craft myself. During my brief stint as a magazine editor, the parent company of the firm I worked for owned the rights to the Hank Jansen name. Jansen was a mythical English journalist who had become a Chicago newshound; during my art school days and before, his relatively mild exploits had acquired a brief notoriety. Many writers had had the job of supplying them; the current incumbent, a small, genial Yorkshireman who had never been to America and didn't want to, nonetheless took the Chicago papers on a weekly basis. He was a mine of information on all matters affecting City Hall; political appointments, scandals, and the rest. He also had holes in his shoes; he was knocking out the titles on a monthly basis for a hundred pounds a time, sale of copyright. With Christmas coming on, he admitted he was a little pushed. I bearded the Gold boys in their den. He had several children; couldn't they see their way clear to helping out a little, for his family's sake if not for him?

Like the good East End lads they were, they saw the point at once. They raised the rate to a hundred and twenty. The recipient was pathetically grateful. He insisted we go out for a drink. "After all, Mr. Roberts, you're a real writer. I'm not in your class; wouldn't pretend to be."

I rise in my wrath. There's a verb in every sentence; and there's a plot, with a beginning, a middle, and an end. I've read a damned sight worse, from people who fancied themselves mightily; how he does it on a non-stop basis defeats me. Agreed, the material isn't to my taste; but that's beside the point. "I'll have a drink with you any time you like, Henry; but it'll be on me. You're the writer; I just make patterns round the edges...."

The old warehouse, just across the road from Cable Street, stays strongly in my mind. Outside stood one of those massive, inimitable London pillar boxes; one slot for local letters, another for the rest of the world. Within, lost amid floor after floor stacked with imported magazines, a little printing press thumped day after day, blocking out the dollar prices on the mags with their sinister titles—*Man's Fury*, *Man's Revenge*, and a whole lot besides—and substituting shillings and pence. The video nasties have taken over now; but in the late sixties that sort of material was still very much the province of the printed page.

The Christmas of Henry's raise was my first and last with the firm. My mag was folding; some jobrackers had taken the Gold boys for an alleged ten grand, savings had to be made. And I had no stomach for the rest of their operations. Nonetheless, it seems a gesture of some sort is called for. After all they have been more than fair to me, according to their lights. I approach Mr. Ralph.

"Look, I've more or less finished up. The copy for the last issue's with the printers; and I don't like twiddling my thumbs. How about a firm's Christmas card?"

He narrows his eyes. "Don't know about that, Mr. Roberts. Never done one of those. What would it cost?"

"Don't be daft. You're paying me to the end of the year; I'm just sitting there now. I'd be using your time up."

The idea takes hold. "Who'd print it though, Mr. Roberts? Who'd print it for us?"

"There's Ken upstairs; I'm sure he'd jump at the chance. Have to lay his hand on a bit of decent paper stock; but that shouldn't be a problem. You've got it made...."

The printer, a perky, cheerful man, scratches his head. "I dunno. Never done anything like that. Line block you reckon? Just one color?"

"Dead simple. You'd do it standing on your head. Better than knocking price changes out; it must drive you round the twist." He's a brother-in-law of the Golds; in typical Jewish fashion, they set him up with his first machine. He told me some time back he was hoping to move out eventually, start on his own. He's already picking up a little work on the side; which is why he has been able to take on a lad. He's still uncertain though. "You reckon we could do it then? What sort of a drawing would it be?"

I point. "That's a printing press; and you're a printer. Leave the rest to me. There won't be any problems, I'll give you camera-ready art. Come on, Ken; you can make it your first real job."

"We'll have a go," he says. "Can't do more." He looks thoughtful. "I know where I can get hold of a nice bit of paper. Bloke just round the corner. White cartridge, you reckon?"

I make tracks. I've got things to do myself. Like sorting out a design, fast.

The printer's lad pounds up the outside fire escape. He lays the first proof on the table. "There you are. What you reckon?" He turns the paper over, angles it to the light to show the pressure was correct. "Look at that," he says proudly. "No imprint...."

Getting the drawing out on time was a bit of a hassle. I decided the Pool of London was a natural; after all, it's only down the road. But the huge subject was daunting; a decorative treatment not only seemed called for, it was a virtual necessity. Though I got a fair amount of stick for it in my local; the Garrick, next door to the old Leman Street nick. "Tower Bridge ain't like that," says the landlord. "Why'd you bend it in the middle?"

"It was the only way I could fit it in. Like using a camera with a fisheye lens."

He takes the point at once. But a fresh complaint arises from the regulars. Why didn't I tell them about it sooner? They would have bought some; and Bill could have sold them behind the bar. Gone well, they would have.

It isn't my card; it belongs to the firm. I'm still cheered though. I feel the thing has passed a major test. It's to do with London; and Londoners accepted it.

A certain amount of mirth is evinced in Dock Street. A Christmas card, from Gold Star Books? It comes to Mr. Ralph's ears eventually. He is vaguely indignant; certainly he doesn't see why there should be amusement. After all, everybody sends Christmas cards; so why shouldn't they? It's a proper Christian thing to do.

There's an odd little sequel. Almost on my last day, I'm called down to the office. To my surprise I'm introduced to a quiet, slim man in a dogcollar. It's the vicar of St. Mary's, the church just across the road. He has a good name in the district; he leaves the building open nights for the drifters who are always moving through the area, and seems to have no problems as a result. He much admires the drawing I did; if I have no objections, he would like to use it on the cover of his parish magazine. Would it be possible to buy the block? So Mr. Ralph still hasn't understood. So shrewd in other matters; but this is out of his league.

"But I told you, Ralph. The job was done in the company's time. So the drawing's yours, and the plate. It's nothing to do with me."

He considers for a moment. Then he hands the zinco to the vicar with a flourish, and solemnly shakes hands. It's a last and somehow curiously apt memory of six months I wouldn't have missed.

Other recollections of the time abound of course. One of the few publications the company actually produced for itself was a pallid and sporadic little girlie book to which, in the manner of later times, readers were invited to contribute. The result was a continual stream of submissions, some eminently forgettable, others of considerable merit. One series of photographs stays in my mind. The model was blonde, and ravishing. She was shaved; and although each pose was perfectly modest and proper, she was eminently—the polite way to put it would be *visible*. Very occasionally, one comes across a figure of that type; anatomy is endlessly variable, never more so than with regard to the human female. It was Mr. Ralph's habit to check all potential material for possible offence; any details he deemed unsuitable he would rub at vigorously with his thumb, as though the act itself would expunge the unwanted item. "That'll have to go, Mr. Roberts," he would say, clicking with his tongue. "That'll have to go...." His attitude to his chosen trade of soft porn was one I found intriguing. He genuinely considered the human body obscene *per se*, which I did not; on the other hand, business was business.

The new entry for the glamour stakes attracted his attention at once; immediately, his thumb began to make its habitual circling motions. He knew a bloke round the corner as well, in this case a retoucher; the prints were spirited away for his attentions. When they returned a day or so later the inevitable had happened; the model has been de-sexed, her body was as bland and featureless as that of a shop window dummy. I shook my head. "These pictures weren't obscene before, Ralph; they were beautiful. But they're obscene now...."

He glances at me and at the prints, head on one side and lips pursed slightly. Then he shakes his head, and slips them back into their folder. Never will he understand these artist blokes; not to his dying day.

On Sunday nights, it seemed the clan repaired to their local boozer; there, aided by a liberal supply of ale, ideas for new business ventures flowed thick and fast. On Monday mornings I was generally the recipient; Ralph would appear upstairs, bubbling over with this scheme or that. On one memorable occasion he proposed a notion for a new glossy mag that would take the publishing world by storm. SF and fantasy stories would be its staple fare, blended with an admixture of high class erotica. Oddly enough, Bonfiglioli had had a very similar thought; it had always been dear to his heart. "I saw this picture," said Ralph, eyes gleaming at the memory. "In one o' the supplements, it was. There were these two birds, in this coach. One o' them had got the top of her dress undone; and the other—you won't believe this, Mr. Roberts—the other was *squeezing her titty*." As a matter of fact I knew the painting, or had seen it reproduced; it's a good example of the mild, or sometimes not so mild, erotica beloved by the Victorians.

He steps back triumphantly. "That's the sort o' thing we shall be wanting from you," he says. "I mean, that is filth. No question. It's filth; but it's art...."

I shake my head. The idea is sound enough; but with no staff, no up-front money for little things like reproduction fees and equipment that consists of a rickety table, a typer and a pair of rusty scissors, there is nothing to be done. I wished it had been possible though; in a way I still do. As it is, all that's left is a single glowing phrase; it would make a handy title for somebody's autobiography sometime. "It's filth; but it's art...."

I am to hear Mr. Ralph's dulcet tones just once more; some years later, by sheer chance, I catch a radio interview with him. The subject is the latest of the short-lived peccadillos that in a way were his publishing lifeblood. Faced with the suggestion that he has overstepped the mark, he is properly indignant. "No, no, no. We keep the right side of the line, always have. There's just one thing. The *line* keeps *moving*...."

Not long after, news came that he had been killed in a light plane crash. My sorrow was genuine and deep. *Shalom*, Ralph.

Professionalism, or honesty, can be an Achilles heel. The artwork I produced for my magazine covers never reappeared upstairs. The typescripts and layouts, yes; but not the art. I assumed it was being filed. Twenty years later, in Glasgow of all places, I find it was being spirited away and auctioned at Conventions; for relatively high prices too, considering the time. I make a belated mental note. My expertise in the matter of London and a few other places might be a subject for debate; but despite all, I'm still definitely wanting in the ways of thieves. Somehow, I lack the proper mental makeup.

My Christmas in Town was notable for a number of things, apart from the demise of the mag and Henry's raise. The kneesup at the Garrick stays particularly in mind; the place packed to overflowing, the hubbub of voices, rumbling of the ancient, detuned piano in the corner of the bar. It was being driven—that really seems the only word—by a thin, morose-looking man wearing a bowler and a long and shapeless mac. A cargo of pints, bought presumably to ensure the performer's continued vigor, stood atop the piano; and one of its legs was definitely on a dodgy board because with every extra-heavy thump it swayed alarmingly, sending rivulets of beer coursing down its battered front to vanish between its yellowed teeth. Apart from their gross flatness, the sounds it was emitting were extraordinary. I admired the player's pro-gressiveness for a time; then I noticed a musical colleague was hunched at the bar, shoulders shaking and tears coursing down his face. I asked what the music was; I had taken it to be late Bartók.

"As a matter of fact, you'll find it's 'Down at the Old Bull and Bush.' But he's playing in two different keys and two different tempi. Let not the left hand know what the right hand doeth...."

Oh, well. Later, when the merriment subsides, they'll have a brick heaved through the Saloon Bar door. It happens regularly, and invariably on Saturday nights. The landlord never bothers having the new panes puttied in; he has fitted snibs to the frame instead, and keeps a spare stock of glass. I asked him once why the great frosted panels that front the place are spared, with their curlicued Victorian motifs; he explained that the locals take care to miss them, they know they are ir-replaceable. "It's a sort o' natural courtesy...."

Oh well again. I shall miss the place myself; the bookies' shops, the fat pillar boxes, even the dried honk outside Aldgate East tube station on Monday mornings. Invariably, it seemed to be studded with prawns. And telling Arnold, the most misanthropic West Indian I ever met, to piss off when he started his weekly winge about the black man having no chance. They're not all light-hearted singers of calyp-sos; but *ex Londinia, semper aliquid novi.*

There's a further faint echo of my last Dock Street job. In the runup to their launch, the Kerosina mob come up with a bright idea. Would it be possible to produce some prints of the new frontispiece? They could sell them in the Book Room, as part of the promotion.

Anything's possible. It's just that I don't rate their chances very much. After all, it's only a drawing; they're dead boring. And it's not in color. It would be better if it was colored; and you know, sort of finished smooth. Airbrushed art is always better; it's cleverer. I go along with it though. After all, an idea is an idea; and they haven't come up with that many. Constructive ones at least. I ring one of the top platemaking firms in Town. I happen to know the boss; my colleague has been using his services for years. His van picks up regu-larly round Waitrose-on-Thames; also, it would be fitting if the last touch to Kaeti's promotion was supplied by London.

There have been hiccups on this job from day one. Hardly surprising, considering the general circumstances; some jobs are like

that though. Next morning I only leave the studio for a few minutes;
but it's enough. The landlady's daughter sends the driver away when
he comes to collect the artwork. She thinks he looks a little rough;
also, he says something about a plate. She doesn't want to buy any
plates, she has a cupboard full of them. I'm reduced to drumming my
fingers; but my colleague, as ever, is phlegmatic. They'll be back;
once a London process house sniffs a job, they don't give up that easily.

He's right of course. Next day, the yellow van with its well-
remembered logos reappears. The driver laughs at the look on my face.
I hand the job over. He asks what I want, litho or line block.

"I said I'd leave it to Mr. Keene."

He grins again. Not much doubt what the answer will be. The
head of the firm is wedded to the old techniques, now rapidly passing
from the scene; but there never was a spirit ink yet that gave you a solid
black. Also, on one visit to his premises I caught my foot on the frame
of an old hand press, stacked dismantled in a corner.

"Good God, an Albion. Haven't used one since I was at art
school...."

The proprietor, a large, vivacious man, snorted. "Bleedin'
hell, they all say that. Everybody that comes in. Quarter of a million,
that thing next door set me back. Lasers, the lot. Won't even let me
near. And what do they come out with, every time? 'Look, an old Albion....'"

"Sorry. I just go back too far. Etching and Dragon's Blood
and all that stuff."

He darts into a small side room, reappears with a jar of the
dark red resin. The last time I used it was to stop the bite on a handmade line plate. "Dragon's Blood," he says, with the air of making a
point.

When the parcel is delivered from Town I instantly feel the
weight of the big zinco inside. I carry it up to my studio, open it carefully, sniff the fresh, sharp scent of new ink. There's magic in it. A
rough magic, no doubt; after all, there's not a pushbutton in sight. But
it suits me.

I don't check the backs of the sheets for imprint. I know there
won't be any. But for a moment the shadow of Ken's lad is definitely
at my elbow.

After my magazine session I took home with me, among other
things, a dose of mumps. I had been half expecting it; a minor epi-
demic was flourishing at the time, and it was about the only childhood
blessing I had not enjoyed. I knew what was often said about adult
complications; fortunately, they don't take place. Instead, Lemady appears in my sick room. She wears a crisp white uniform; she has just
emerged from her own little surgery along the corridor. She makes up

what she calls a PTR chart, pins it over the bed. When he arrives, the doctor looks at it curiously. "Who did that?"

"A friend of mine."

"Hmm. You have some very efficient friends."

That's right enough at least. In more ways than one.

I'm driving down the big hill into Marlborough. A snow-plough has been through, to clear a narrow track. To either side, the piled drifts are higher than the Spitfire's roof. Despite my best efforts, the car wags solemnly from side to side across the residue of icy slush.

I'm following a massive low loader carrying tarpaulined cable drums. It pulled out of a layby halfway down the hill. I glance at the rear view mirror and cringe mentally. There was a pair of them; and his mate came out behind me. All I can see now is a broad, yellow-striped bumper. I just hope they're both good drivers; otherwise I'm going to finish up as a singularly unappetizing jam sarnie.

I make the broad main street eventually. A snowdrift in the middle looks suddenly inviting. I signal frantically and head for it. As the second truck passes, the driver grins and puts his thumb up. I'm glad somebody found it a rewarding experience.

I was mad to try it of course. But Christmas is close again, and Lemady has set her heart on a handmade mixing bowl in one of the town's numerous gift shops. Anyway, the reports had said the snow was farther west.

The A4 was clear almost to the Savernake forest; but then the problems began. I make the purchase, head for the big restaurant they still call The Polly. Somehow though I don't fancy the idea of one of their famous Victorian breakfasts. The deviled kidneys would remind me too sharply I still have to attempt the journey home.

Repacking the bowl next day, I can't resist a large last-minute inscription. HOLY GRAIL—USE NO HOOKS. After all, if you're going to be as crazy as that it's fitting to mark the event in some small way. But Arthur's lot were fall guys as well, when you think it through. So at least I'm in good company.

* * * * * *

Perhaps it's time for an *entr'acte*.

When I was working in Maidenhead we were blessed with a pert young secretary who in addition to her other qualities possessed the rare virtue of literacy. One day she typed up a piece of copy for me, and brought it through for me to check. At one point I had used the construction "alright." I noticed she had typed it as two words. I hadn't been too sure about it myself; after all, "already" is accepted, as is "altogether." I mentioned it to her, more, truly, to get her opinion than in criticism. Her response was to march out of the studio. She returned carrying a small book, which she placed on my drawing board. "If you can find it in that," she snapped, "I'll type it. Otherwise, I won't."

I looked. "That" was the pocket *Oxford*. I hemmed. "You're quite right, my dear," I said. "I promise I won't do it again."

I looked round. To my surprise, my colleague of the time was still uncurling himself. He said he had thought the roof would blow off.

"Good heavens, no. The girl was right, I was wrong." I had remembered an injunction somewhere in Fowler's sacred pages. "Don't improvise...." Neither have I again; all these years later, when I come to use the phrase I remember with a wry smile, and write two words.

In *The Summing Up*, Somerset Maugham recounts a not dissimilar story about a typist who took it on her to correct his work. I would imagine the main difference was sartorial. Our lass wore extremely frank minis, and had an equally forthright way of bending down to the filing cabinet. I often wondered what happened to her; any young woman who wore bright red knickers and kept the *Oxford Dictionary* by her typewriter, seemed bound for an interesting future.

VIII.

I ease the car across the yard, following the flickering hurricane lamp. Despite the surrounding outbuildings, the wind still rocks the Spitfire on its springs; and there's half an inch of water in the foot wells. It has rained solidly from first light; I had wanted to push on further, but a few miles from Oban I decided I had had enough.

The garaging, an old stable block, is dry and spacious; and they have already told me they will not be charging extra. It's the end of the season, there are few other guests; it will be best to have the motor under cover for the night.

I collect my bag, follow my oilskinned host back the way we had come. Drifts of rain show fleetingly, lit by the hotel windows. I'm shown to a pleasant little room. I lie on the bed for a while and smoke a cigarette. It's been a long haul from Waitrose-on-Thames. Lemady always promised she would show me Scotland; but that won't happen now. So I came on my own.

Downstairs, I find as expected I'm too late for dinner; or rather, the famous Scottish High Tea. The housekeeper, a refugee surely from Dr. Finlay's establishment, is already putting her coat on to go home. Despite my protests she insists on preparing food. It is a cold night, and the young man has come a long way. He will be needing something warm inside him.

The meal, an excellent mixed grill, is served by a tall, saturnine man with what I can only describe as a lived-in face. He slams the plate onto the table with a species of quiet vehemence. Later I find my way to the bar. It's a wide, welcoming room, paneled and beamed. Stuffed salmon line the walls; and there are dour pictures of the anglers, each with his hand on the shoulder of his ghilly. It's so much as expected, it might be a film set; but it's not.

The daunting waiter is now performing the function of a barman. He has changed his jacket, from dark blue to maroon; but it's the only detectable difference. As before, he glowers at me.

I was hoping to stay here for a day or so at least. So it would make sense to try and get on friendly terms. I ask him if he would like a drink with me. He places his hands flat on the copper bar top, barks, "I willna," and stalks out. His voice has a hard, Glaswegian edge; very different from the whispering of the locals.

Oh, well. At least I tried.

The barman is back. He's carrying a couple of pints of foaming McEwan's Export in one large fist. He slams them onto the bar, fixes me with another of his inimitable stares. "I wouldna drink with you, because you're drinking with me...."

I turn away, look back to the pictures of the long-gone anglers. I'm wondering if there's something in the Sight thing after all. Certainly this unlikely-seeming man divined that at heart I was not too happy. And I wasn't making a feature of it; apart from anything else, I was too glad to get in out of the wet, find a bed for the night. I've received other impressions of Scotland since of course, that's bound to happen; but they do say the first time counts for most. After all, you can only get a first impression once.

My new friend's name is Stevie. He introduces me to his partner in crime, a slim blond lad currently reading Theology at Edinburgh. In Stevie's view that seems to impart a vaguely sinister overtone. Or maybe it's the gambler's bootlace ties Iain habitually sports. No other guests appear; so we solemnly toast each other. Then England, Scotland, and various points of the compass. The evening doesn't exactly turn into a *celidh* but it's something not far removed. The party breaks up in the wee small; but not before a mysterious stranger has come tapping at the side door. A consignment of fish is borne away swiftly into the nether regions of the place. Later I pluck the courage to ask about the seeming gift.

"Stevie, your menu. Poached Loch Awe salmon. Does it mean what it says, or...." I make vague gestures suggestive of scrambling or running.

As ever, he is equal to the occasion. He draws himself up. "It covers evra' contingency," he assures me solemnly. So everything Compton Mackenzie talked about is true; not that I ever doubted it.

There is a raw edge to the barman/waiter's humor. I discover it by degrees. He had been planning to go up to Portree; something to do with a car deal in which he has become involved. He put the trip off though. An old injury is playing him up; he has enough steel in his leg apparently to make a fair-sized model of the Forth Bridge. He's better now; except he's peeing blood. It's another small problem he has.

"Good God...."

He assures me cheerfully it's of no importance. It happens from time to time; all in all, he's a fair physical wreck. And the symptoms have their amusing aspects. Not long back for instance, he startled the punters in a public loo. The discolored stream passed down the channel at their feet; but he was quick to reassure them. "Don't worry, fellers," he roared. "It's on'y me...."

I drain my glass. Suddenly my problems, even Lemady's distress, seem a long way away. What we need now really is an aniline screen; the sort the fantasy people use.

I'd planned to make the crossing to Iona. After all, everybody does. Or so I've read. I drive back down to Oban to book the trip. By ferry to Mull, a coach across the island; the last stage is handled by a local family, it is not included in the ticket. Packed lunches will be available though.

Stevie is mightily impressed. He imparts the news to his colleague. "Iain, he's awa' on a MacBraine's boat. Then he's awa' on a MacBraine's coach. And he thinks...." He pounds the counter top, begins to roar with laughter. "He thinks he's comin' *back*...." Nonetheless, he makes a bet with me. Iona is well known to be a dry island; it was one of the provisions made when it was gifted to the Scottish Church. But if I don't make the crossing in the company of a crate of whisky, he will buy me a pint. And *vice versa*.

"But there's three boats a day. Or is it four?"

He nods solemnly. He is aware of that; the wager still stands.

The day is bright and sunny, the narrow stretch of water between Mull and Columba's island seemingly flat calm; but the sturdy open boat still rolls and bounces. A girl is in charge of it. She wears jeans and an old shirt; a shawl is draped loosely round her shoulders. She grips the long tiller easily; wavy chestnut hair blows round her face, and her feet are bare. Lemady would be intrigued. She often told me how she would go out with the fishing boats, when she was a girl herself; the crews would throw crabs down onto the bottom boards, to make her skip.

Watching the craft approach the little jetty, I had thought my bet secure. At the last moment though a saloon car appeared, seemingly from nowhere. A young man in a white steward's jacket handed down not one crate of whisky, but two. Flora MacDonald threw a square of tarpaulin casually across them; but the musical clinking of the bottles can still be heard. I shall lose out twice then; because as ever, Facts are there to be reported.

In front of the Abbey stands one of those tall, immensely thin Celtic crosses. The sockets on the stubby arms once held wooden extensions, to give the thing a more normal proportion during services. In later times, the wind still raged at it; the Devil huffed and puffed so mightily he broke it clean across. So they took the relic to the mainland; what stands in its place is a reinforced concrete copy. There are ways and means of ensuring the triumph of the Faith.

The Old Man was hyperactive here by all accounts. Maybe he was annoyed by the constant stream of piety. A monk, watching the West Door from a squint set in the wall, once saw him enter the church, and begin to climb toward him. Wisely, the Brother exited through the tiny window; but he was a well-built man. As he scrabbled for a purchase, his fingers scratched deep grooves in the stonework of the surround; they can be seen to this day.

Roofless for many years before its restoration, the shell of the church was overgrown with moss and lichens. A trace of their presence remains; an intense viridian stain. In the nave, there's a feeling of being beneath the sea. I'm to encounter such an effect again; at Muckross, in Ireland. But not for a year or so.

Outside, a Brother passes, seeming lost in contemplation. He is sandalled and bearded; a grey robe flaps round his ankles. On the mainland, I asked Stevie what the Community people were really like. He looked thoughtful for a moment; but his answer was inimitable. "Pairmanently sozzled...." Perhaps though the young man is drunk with more than the Water of Life. We must not be waspish; after all, this is a place of charity.

Iain develops a spluttering head cold. He gets his friend to drive him down to the local doctor. The Glaswegian comes back grinning broadly. The lad's a head case sure enough. Worse than him.

"Why? What happened?"

Outside the surgery, apparently, is a little cemetery. The suffering theologian nods toward it. "Ye'd best drop me here, Stevie. I see he has a waiting room." The macabre humor of the Celts strikes again. It would make a handy line for a story. Best not tell the fans though. You're supposed to make it all up out of your head; otherwise it's cheating.

It's probably fairer to say certain fans. And they're maybe not wholly to blame. After all, it's not their fault the word is short for fanatic.

The couple of days stretch to a week. It's time to head back; it can't be put off any longer. One thing I'm determined on though. On my last morning, I order salmon. I've never tasted the like before, and probably never will again. They throw the steaks into a dry pan atop the Aga, for them to cook in their own juice; the result is exquisite. Stevie though looks mournful when he serves the meal. In place of the usual goodly collop are two smaller, thicker portions. He apologizes for them. "If ye ken my problem; it's concairned with the anatomy of the fush...." So I've eaten my way down to the wrist. I was hoping the thing would last out; it did, but only just.

I pay my bill, drive round to the front of the hotel. The omnipresent Stevie fills the tank for me. As I pull away I seem to hear a distant jangling. Maybe it's the tills of Waitrose-on-Thames, calling me back. Not for a wedding though. Unlike the tills you could hear from Llareggub Hill; but that's only a fantasy.

Years later, I ring the hotel on impulse. I've decided I'd like to go back; see the place, and the area, just once again. I'm answered by an urbane English voice. The establishment is under new management; I am assured I will find things much changed. None of the folk I might have met on my former visit are there; and certainly none of the staff.

I put the phone down gently. So it was a Halfway House after all; somehow I always suspected it.

When a biologist wants to know what bugs are floating about, he drops a spot of nutrient onto an agar dish. Then he leaves it on the window sill, and counts the moulds that grow. The comparison is hardly flattering, but much the same thing happens when a book is produced. Or any artefact, I suppose. One thinks first of the editors, their secretaries and assistants; because of course these are the folk you see. But there are many more. The publisher's readers, and, God save the Mark, advisers; the graphics department, if the company aspires to such pretensions, the blurb writers and production people. The folk who clean the offices of commerce ought to be included; as they were, intriguingly, on a limited-edition book I saw once. Plus the critics and reviewers who wait, pens poised for mayhem. I've been asked the odd time where I thought I would be without them. It's a good question; where would they be though, without their supply of cannon fodder?

Over all of course are the shadowy Directors of the Company. One seldom encounters such exalted folk; though I was allowed the brief use of a Boardroom once. The decorators were in; my editor of the time had been kicked out of his office, it was the only room available for our deliberations. We sat at each end of the imposing table, shouted insults to each other and skidded sheafs of quarto forward and back. It put me in mind of the process used to age examination sketchbooks at art school. The rules stated they must be real working specimens; so after we had selected the best sheets and rebound them we would sit in pairs in the big general purpose studio and sling them to each other across the floor till the new card covers looked honorably worn. The effect was highly artistic.

If one adds the salesmen who traipse round with their bundles of cover flats, the drivers who fulfill the orders and of course collect the returns, then the jobrackers, the booksellers, and their assistants, the ring of mold spores starts to look extensive. And before that of course comps have had to set the job, process men have made the plates, somebody has done the makeready on the presses. There'll be the printers and their lads, after them the binders; somebody has to pay for the Christmas wayzgoose, and it's starting to look like you. But it's far from finished yet. "Don't forget they'll all have accountants," says a friend whose mind runs along such lines. Of course; and they'll have staff as well. I had forgotten; but my brain doesn't usually work that way.

Once ingested by the system, the spot of nutrient starts to look vanishingly small. It's best to call attention to it, or yourself. Become a Joiner, that's one hopeful way; it has nothing to do, apparently, with the working of wood. Infiltrate some literary parties, whatever they might be, attend all the book launches going; you never know, you might meet someone you can butter up. I tried that though; leastways, I got stuck with one or two launches. They had a certain grinding sameness. A roomful of earnest people, standing too close to each other and talking at high volume; a geriatric recordplayer competing with the din; a stack of empty plates, because the sarnies have already been scoffed, some large cans of lager on the side, a grudging pipkin of beer. Usually with a languid character draped in the vicinity, expounding on the joys of English ale. Five minutes of that and I was already edging for the door.

Most of the aspiring wordsmiths are going to be ripped off. After all, it happens to bigger folk than they'll ever be. In the course of an interview, Joseph Heller observes sardonically that if anybody imagines he made a nickel out of *Catch-22* they'd best think again. I'm hardly surprised; the first patronizing contract would have taken ample care of that. Later it would have been a different story; but the publishing trade always was quick on the draw with its prayer mats.

The partygoers will never admit their downfall though; not to the fans, the critics, and ten times over, never to each other. Or somebody might take the chance to put the boot in, tread you a little farther down the stack. Individually, they'll all be making fortunes; or doing their best to suggest it. So the truth will never out; they can't afford to come clean.

My landlady once owned a poodle that yapped. It barked from morning to night; whenever she took a swipe at it, it would run behind her husband's legs and a row would ensue. It was a good ploy; it worked every time. There was just one thing; it meant the dog was smarter than the humans. It's a pity that writers are so easy to defeat in detail; but they've only got their vanity to thank.

A taste for decent ale always was my downfall. But not in the way that might immediately be supposed. While working in the Thames Valley, I'm taken out to lunch by the boss of the time. He's a graceless, dishonest little lout; the very sort that gives advertising a bad name. Why my presence was required I have no idea; he surely can't be expecting me to add a little tone. Though admittedly any conversation would be an improvement on his.

We're joined by an executive, so-called, from Town. Another very partial youth. I can't see him surviving in any sort of trade for long; but you can never tell. Some of these folk have hidden depths of sycophancy. He rhapsodizes at length on the delights of country living. Which is fine till the beer arrives; in half pint pewter tankards, to add insult to injury. The executive slurps his with apparent relish; I ask the barmaid to take mine away. The bitter has turned to a sort of noisome malt vinegar; the stink from it is getting to me. The hotel is famous, both in the area and farther afield; which is obviously just as well. No landlord I know would dare serve such muck in his Public Bar; quite rightly, the customers would throw it at his head.

We repair to the terrace. The area is currently suffering a singularly sticky heatwave. Things are scarcely improved by the operations of a couple of unmuffled jackhammers, working across the courtyard. So haven't the operators heard of lunch breaks?

A second beer arrives. If anything it's worse than the first. "Get it down yer," snarls my employer, with a species of urgency. Obviously he's afraid of creating a bad impression; particularly as the nitwit across the table is still burbling about the glories of Real Ale. I can't oblige though. Even if I could force the stuff past my teeth, there would be horrendous consequences. Seasoned drinkers have several flamboyant ways of describing them; but enough of that. Suffice to say that I would be rather ill.

The Assistant Manager of the place floats forward on a cloud of mingled unction and irritation. There seems to be some dissatisfaction; what would seem to be the problem?

My temper has snapped though. It was the jackhammers that caused it really; so perhaps I'm noise-sensitive as well. "The problem is this muck you're serving instead of beer. Will you take it off the table please? I've already sent one lot away; if I have to smell it any more I shall throw up...."

Obviously the situation can't be saved. I may even have lost my employer an account. Not that that will worry him for long. He never services them anyway. When one falls off the shelf he just sticks a new one on the other end and moves the files along; the name of the game is getting a nice retainer up front. Then it doesn't matter. In any case he was getting set to fire me. The artwork I'm doing will be blamed; the artwork is always blamed, it's the one thing that can't be quantified. Particularly if you don't know which way up to hold it. I decide I'm just not cut out for trade; not his sort at least. Book launches would be preferable; though given the chance I'd prefer to opt for neither.

Jenny, the daughter of my Maidenhead colleague, works at the noisome hotel for a time. As a schoolgirl she was shy, almost mousey; but a sea change has been wrought. She has become very beautiful; I tell her as much, and she thanks me solemnly. In Town one day with her folks, she stares up thoughtfully at the great bulk of the Opera House. "I've always fancied going there. There wouldn't be much point though; it's all in foreign languages."

A thought comes to me. "Do you reckon? How about you all coming as my guests? I'll try and find something."

If things are worth doing, they're worth doing well. I try my best, even down to chocolates for the ladies. Jenny sits awestruck, the light from the great stage reflecting on her solemn face. Peter Grimes staggers through the swirling fog. Sung by the Welshman Robert Tear, the role has acquired a new and startling dimension; the misanthropic fisherman has become a dangerous, frightened child. The score ends on its three massive, muffled heartbeats; with accustomed mordant humor, Peter once assured me the day I dared to start the applause there would be four.

On the drive home, the new young theatregoer partly recovers the power of speech. "You wait till Monday. Wait till I tell them I've been to the Opera...."

She's a waitress now at a swep-up local restaurant. She told me once, on Mondays the clientele boast to each other of their weekend exploits. I've come across establishments like that; Waitrose-on-Thames specializes in them. The distance traveled seems to be of primary importance. "Overall, I did about a thousand miles. Picked up fifty K of business; so I suppose you could say it was worth it...."

"No, you mustn't say that. Just tell them you went to the Garden. Some fool's bound to ask which one; you look down your nose and say, 'Covent Garden, of course....'"

When I meet her some time later she chuckles at the memory. The dialogue went word for word as I predicted. A shame one has to descend to such depths; but faced with idiots, there's no option. It's all they understand.

I took back something different from the evening. Significant experiences can be savored, and magic memories created, without the strict need for erotic involvement. Something I always knew of course; but it's nice to be reassured.

Artwork can be a source of piquant problems. When I was working in Reading, my autocratic employer always took pride in writing any instructions to the blockmakers himself. Not that they needed them; for the most part they could see what was wanted at a glance. Nonetheless, systems are there to be observed. One day I overhear the great man discussing some infraction with the boss of the local process house. Not that I'm exactly eavesdropping. His office is at the other end of the corridor; but when he's on the phone, particularly when he's piqued, the whole building is made aware. "You're not

paid to think," he roars finally. "Just follow your instructions...."
And the handset is slammed down.

A day or so later a most curious block turns up at the Agency.
My employer is puzzled. "There's supposed to be two of these. It's
supposed to be red and black. You should have done two drawings."
"I did. One on board, see, the other as an overlay. He's made
them as one plate."
"What? Why should he do a damn fool thing like that?"
I lift the top sheet. "No instructions. I suppose he didn't realize." For once, my employer havers. "Oh. Well, go up and see
him. Sure you'll sort something out...." I exit sympathetically. After
all, he's only been trading since the Thirties. You can't expect him to
grasp all the technicalities at once.

The platemaker, a large, amiable man—leastways, he's always
been amiable to me—shakes his head sorrowfully. "These things happen now and then. Supposed to be two plates, was it? He never
said...."
"I know. And you're not paid to think." I pick up one of the
proofs. "Nice job though; wouldn't have thought you'd have got it as
sharp as that through Kodatrace."
"Yeah," he says, "come out well. We were surprised ourselves." He shakes his head. "We shall just have to make a couple
more. Cost a bob or two though, being a half page. Zinc's just gone
up again." He opens the drinks cupboard. "What are you having?"

The Keroseenies, as they dubbed themselves in a moment of
rare wit, decide to branch out. They won't be using me for their next
offering. They want a real artist; someone who doesn't draw in pencil
first. They're pleased enough with the results of their initiative till they
get the bill for the wrapper; then the feathers begin to fly a little. Why
is it so high? It's over double any of mine.
"They made a four-color set. Only thing they could do. Matter of fact I was thinking of using four-color next time myself."
"You can't! We can't afford it! You'll have to do that...
whatever it is you do!"
I had been using color line, hand-separated. I was going to do
the same again anyway. It's part of the house style I created for them.
Not that I suppose most of them have realized they possess such a
thing. After all, it's only graphics; that sort of stuff's dead boring.
Unless you can push the buttons for yourself.

When I did my Nat. Dip., illustrators had a bible of their own:
Processes of Graphic Reproduction, by Harold Curwen. The printing
trade has changed a lot since those days; but the basic principles remain. I've been told since times enough, you never learn a useful thing
at art school. In my case at least it wasn't so. Though the first time I

prepared artwork for real I did have the odd qualm. My first employer didn't exactly help. The job was a firm's Christmas card, three-color; he peered at the overlays suspiciously. "Do you actually know what you're doing?" The work completed, he did his well known jaw-clenching act. "Tell me something I've never actually been sure of. Is line block a *photographic* process?"

I did blink a little. After all, he'd been a national cartoonist for years enough. It was the first time I'd realized that sort of amateurism isn't restricted to people who don't get paid.

I'm chatting to a pleasant enough lad who told me he's doing some sort of design course. One of the new color newspapers has just come out; one of the shorter-lived examples. I shake my head. "I don't go much on that. That register's out by an eighth of an inch to start with. If I was one of the advertisers I'd want a free insert." He is dismissive though. "I don't know anything about *printing*. My tutor says I don't need to; I'm going to be an Art Director...."

Bemoaning falling standards is a favorite pastime of the not so young. For once though there would seem to be a point. A favored mode of exit from an Agency used to be to pour a cup of tea over the studio manager's head. I can see his baptism already lining itself up. Maybe they do things differently now. Perhaps they'll use a machete. Or an MI6.

In fact the Kerosina masterpiece could have been hand-separated easily enough, had it been worth the effort. The fan room whizz-kid who perpetrated it wouldn't have known what the phrase meant; but maybe that's just as well. It's wrong to inhibit genius with practicalities. Anyway, the author liked it; and he's an Important Man, his name will be an impressive one to drop. True, he stitched them up with an elderly title he hadn't been able to unload anywhere else, exactly as I had said he would; but you have to make allowances for that sort of thing when you're dealing with real talent.

Kerosina was the Wicked Lady from my *Kiteworld* opus, as I have said; her name was formed in the Russian way from that of her husband, who cornered the paraffin market. When the new Company was painfully being set up (pulling it apart again was much more fun), I was formally asked if I would allow its use.

The gaggle of proprietors were vindictive from day one; had they been smart as well they would have realized they could simply lift it. The way the law stands at the moment, book titles and the like are judged too short to be considered individual creative works and so are not afforded copyright. Though if you called your hero Smiley or Bond I'm pretty sure something would be said sooner or later.

The Scottish adventure, and Lemady, are a long way in the past. Or so it seems right now. I'm listening to a denizen of Waitrose-on-Thames detailing events at the town's first Festival; the concert that rounded it off and all the rest. He didn't go of course; he's not into that sort of thing. His girlfriend attended though. She said the audience went dead quiet when the Gershwin thing started. Not a dry eye in the house; or rather on the river bank.

"I can understand that. After a diet of solid punk, I expect even 'Rhapsody in Blue' on a mouth organ would sound pretty spectacular."

I suppose one might say his face darkens. In fact it goes a sort of pale beetroot shade. I'm warned later he intends to sort me out. Leastways that's what he's been giving out round town. I'm not too bothered though. He's one of the little gang who tried to destroy Lucia Queen. On the whole, he's better with distraught blondes.

I'm saved from an untimely fate by the intervention of a kerb. It puts him off physical solutions, for a while at least. He tells all and sundry how it happened. He was walking home from a party, and he tripped somehow; just straightforwardly tripped over. Most unusual; normally he's not a clumsy person at all.

I sympathize. It must have been a rough-hewn piece of street furniture, even for Waitrose-on-Thames, because three contact points are clearly visible; over his eye, on his cheek, and plumb on the point of his jaw. You can even tell something else. That kerb was a south-paw.

So what am I doing here anyway? In this place, at this particular time? It was handy for a while; a good long while, if you add it up. Oxford close, Reading just down the road for art supplies, London not much more than an hour off; at least, till the M25 improved the traffic flow. The Enterprise Culture will be heading this way soon though; the Estate Agencies are already starting to outnumber the shops. There are unisex hairdressers too; while one must never forget the SODC, locally called the Sods. For the most part, the Government grants for Aids relief suffer mysterious deletions; but South Oxfordshire heads the league, it's the only local authority that squirrels away half. Not so much a sign of the times; more an indication that the Thames no longer flows softly. If it ever did. Well, other things being equal the matter's going to be solved for me anyway. And they're getting more equal by the day.

In some ways, Amesbury is a stark little town. An emanation perhaps from the service camps that ring it; Bulford, Lark Hill, and all the rest. On Saturday nights, MPs patrol with the civilian police; Army vehicles shadow the little Skipper buses as they grind up the long hill to the Porton Road, because some of the boy recruits still have to learn the rules. There's magic around though. On the face of things, it may seem a touch unlikely; but magic doesn't necessarily reside in prettiness. It's something Waitrose-on-Thames still has to learn. I found it here once; it's just a case of looking for it again.

An early discovery pleases me. The local Co-Op sells *bootlaces*; on an open shelf as well. That wouldn't do at all, not where I spent my last few years; what would the visitors think? It would create a very bad impression; working class, no less. And there's decorum to be observed in all things. My colleague told me once, when they trade partners in his neck of the woods the white goods go as well; but they do it decently after dark, staggering along like ants with lumps of sugar. Love me, love my Frigidaire. True or not, it makes a good tale; I think though I'll settle for the military shadow.

I'm certainly learning fast. If all else fails, the quickest way to clean a pub loo is with a hand grenade; while the cocking lever of a Stirling is just right for opening Guinness bottles. There's a new world of expertise here, waiting to be tapped.

Tony, the author of the high explosive tale, is assailed by an indignant local. Firing ranges are all very well; but has he thought about the cost to wildlife? How many acres have been desecrated? It's time the Army thought about giving some of it back.

The complainant is distinctly at the wrong address. Tony rises in his wrath. If the other cares to present himself bright and early Sunday morning, he will give him a little tour. He'll show him a dozen places where wild orchids grow in profusion; and a fair amount besides. The Colonel has some unexpected areas of knowledge; but then, you don't make it that far from the ranks in peacetime by growing cabbages. Orchids are another matter.

Hot air balloons, explains Julie crisply, are not what they seemed at first. Fumes from the burning straw sealed the pores of the fabric envelope; trapped products of combustion supplied much of the lift. It's a bit different now; she should know, she flies the things for fun. I glance at her. Her long-tailed eyes are amused. I wonder if all girl aeronautical engineers look like her. I wouldn't know; I never met one before.

So the magic begins. Somehow I was sure it would; it was just a question of having faith. Vivid folk pass through the little town; the place that was old long before Sarum spire raced into the sky. But all things interweave. A Fairy girl might well land by Montgolfier, floating over the big NAAFI warehouse, the ancient plantings that commemorate the Battle of the Nile.

So much for magical maunderings. The next time I meet my Fairy aeronaut she gives me a dirty look.

"I could brain you, Keith. I probably will one day."

"What have I done now?" I'd only just walked in. The matter is simply explained. The last time we chatted we got onto the subject of wines, and the curious English attitude to them. I quoted one of the scriptwriter Denis Norden's most dazzling shafts of wit; the time he translated the name of a singularly noxious brand of fizzy plonk as, "Hurry, I'm going to be sick." Shortly afterward she had gone down to dinner. A family was in residence in the little dining room: Mum, Dad, and a couple of kids. And Dad was a wine expert. He wavered for a long time over the list before settling for the inevitable. Watching him savor it, roll it round his tongue, and extol its virtues was too much. The Fairy fled, leaving her meal unfinished.

Oh well, so much for social chitchat too. It always finishes up getting you into trouble; leastways, that's how it seems to work with me.

It's time maybe for a little reassessment. I lay out my collection of prints. My colleague supplied them, over the years; there are advertising shots and portraits, landscapes, all sorts. There's the old Lamb and Flag in Covent Garden, next to it the Heel Stone from the Rollrights that spooked Lemady so much. I can see why now. There's a brutal quality to the image; sometimes though it's best not to get too creative. You point the camera at what you want, and press the button. You can always be artistic later. The trick is to know when; a touch of hand shading on the enlarger always did work wonders.

"Pubs, Girls and Churches" would be a good title for the collection. At least it describes the contents. There's All Souls, Brixworth for example. One way and another, it's always seemed entwined in my awareness. Sketching it was obligatory in my student days, maybe still is. Driving back from Kettering once, I turned aside; I had asked Peter casually if he would like to see a Saxon church. He admitted later the sight of it took him aback. The great plain nave, a barn for the worship of God, the slim spire the Medievals added; he didn't have wide angle with him, so a virtue was made from necessity. The thing goes soaring out of frame like a dark rocket; I never saw a picture of Brixworth that looked like that. Or any other church.

I'm put in mind of another trip to Brixworth; that time with David, my colleague from the Maidenhead days, a man of deep and proper awareness. I drove on into Northampton to show him the Church of the Holy Sepulchre, grim, Crusader-built, with its round nave, its massive ironstone columns reaching into gloom. He shook his head. "Wouldn't think they're to the same God, would you?"

Driving out of town, I almost bounced off the kerb. The day was bright, the pavements crowded with comely girls in jeans and teeshirts, bright summer frocks. He observed them gravely; mainly, it seemed, the exponents of the cloth *de Nimes*. He has been quiet for some time; finally he delivers his verdict. "Well, mate,I shall remember Northamptonshire for two things. Churches, and bums...."

I wish, not for the first time, that a Boswell-type character could have followed him around as well, to record his throwaway lines. Posterity would have been much enriched.

There's Tammy, brooding on her window seat, toying with her beads. We picked her up from the station, the night we did our twenty-minute shoot. She came blazing along the platform, bronze-tinted hair flying; we wheeled her into a handy hostelry for a relaxer before going on to the flat that was to be our location. An unknown, eyes on the main chance, tried to move in; she dismissed him with a brusqueness of which she was an unconscious mistress. She was already preoccupied with the job ahead. What was this book about, that she was going to help with? What would she have to be?

"Two things really. You could be the hero's girlfriend; she's Scandinavian. Or you could be the ghost that haunts the place. It's someone who lived there in the Thirties."

"Oh..." A quick, unsure grin. "I'll do my best...."

I showed her the contacts in a pub in Waitrose-on-Thames. She had spent the night before with a would-be *inamorato*. The intention was hers, not his. In the morning, he had offered her tea. "I don't like—beep—tea," she yells. Two old ladies start and very nearly drop their cups. Later, my old landlady offers the same very English courtesy. I explain that Tam has strong views about the beverage. It draws an admiring glance.

"You aren't half good with words."

"I'm not the only one."

This time, for once, it is easy for me. I'm not family; I don't have to pick the pieces up, every time she blows her stack. It's the flip side of the father-figure bit; I'm well aware of that. But she was my model; and she did a good job. No point upsetting her now; if there ever was.

Designing the wrapper, my colleague opted for Gill Sans. It's dated now as a typeface; but he was firm. We want a Thirties look, don't we? Then go for it. He was right of course; contrasted with the essential softness of the image, the title line creates a visual shock. Least, it does for those who give such things more than a nano-second of attention. Though he afterward admitted to having had a slight battle with the layout. I allowed myself a faint chuckle.

"Sets wide, don't it?" I should know; I was hand-drawing Gill years before Letraset was thought of. Later, we were spoiled by good ol' Univers. It's something though to be allowed to tackle the problem at all. Under Establishment rules, artist and typographer must never

138

meet. "We don't work that way...." So the illustrator leaves a gap, and hopes, usually in vain, for sympathy. Which is why in the main, crisp packets look better than book wrappers. See the thing as a whole? That's dead old-fashioned. It went out with people like William Morris; whoever he might have been.

Signing the two hundred Specials of *Shades of Darkness* was very evidently the author's first sight of the finished product. Again, the quick double glance told a great deal. "Hmm," said Richard Cowper, that most courteous and urbane of men. "I don't believe I've met this young lady. Would she like one personalized?"

There's Elaine, doing her Maggie Blighe number; and the Clocktower Girl, writhing in hysterical sleep. My colleague moved at high speed to get that shot; he came through the crowd at Knowle Hill at a gallop, like a press man who has scented a story. Surprise was later expressed that I should consider framing the result; but I saw no reason not to. The disturbing piece of photo-journalism had become as all photographs become, a fragment snipped from Time; an Image, to be placed with others.
　　The drawing I finally derived from my colleague's study was the one that won the pot; it was used for the frontispiece of Kaeti's opus. Presented with the award in Birmingham, all I could really think of saying was thank you. I worked on the job for some twenty hours, non-stop. It wasn't a case of hangups; but drawing isn't like riding a bike. Unless practiced regularly, you tend to lose your fist. By the time I had finished scraping back I was prepared to scrap the whole thing and start again, something one never does. Instead, I rang my colleague. I told him I needed some art direction. He arrived an hour later, regarded the thing carefully. Then he took it from me and locked it in his briefcase. He said he would neg it, and let me have a print.
　　"You mean it's finished?"
　　He nodded with equal solemnity. The job was finished.

Here's a change of pace indeed. A five-wheeled bicycle, to coin a solecism; shot at Knowle Hill again, the great steam rally held just outside Reading. Though on that occasion I wasn't present. Next it, an old lady proudly displays her lacework in the Craft Tent. The bobbins she is using make delicate fan shapes, create graceful patterns of their own. I have a feeling I know the camera these were taken with; there's something about the gradation of the tones. I call it the shirt button Leica, because that's about the size of the lens. My colleague found it in a junk shop in Dorset; he'd been looking for a windfall like that since he started taking photographs. Which was at the age of eleven.

Cameras develop personalities of their own. For instance, the next shot was taken with Peter's black-bodied Leica; one of the only models they brought out with that particular finish. A lunchtime customer, late back for the office, hurries down the alleyway beside the Lamb and Flag. As he moves from light to shadow he becomes, momentarily, a threatening silhouette. I had time to take the plastc bag my colleague was carrying; next instant, the image was captured. It was to become the wrapper shot for my long hoped-for ghost collection. "And I beheld the Foul Fiend, coming across the field toward me...." When the prints were first blown up though, something appeared that had been too small to notice on the contacts. Incredibly, angles of incidence and reflection had equaled; an ancient streetlamp overhead had preserved my tiny image. My colleague was unsurprised. "It's the camera. It does that sort of thing...." It's his ghostly camera; point it at any subject, and strange things tend to happen.

That afternoon, magic in retrospect, was one of those times when Images seemed to scatter themselves in my colleague's path like freshly-fallen fruit. A black girl, piquant-faced, glances up at a tall building; for an instant, she has a look of almost comic dismay. Two lasses, out for a day's fun, observe the world from the vantage point of a handy wall; a vivid-faced young woman hefts a shoulder bag and laughs. "A dancer," said Peter decisively; and he was probably right. After all, the Dance Center was just round the corner. And the street performers, the girl with her vaguely Oriental gear; he who is tired of London, sir, is tired of life. As a pundit, Johnson was by no means infallible; though with an anxious little Scot at your elbow, intent on recording every word for posterity, nobody could be expected to win 'em all. But the famous remark holds true.

Here though is the ultimate; the tutelary deity, surely, of that unrepeatable time. She leans against an old wooden barrier; KEEP CLEAR, it proclaims lugubriously. The mass of back-combed hair, the layer on layer of carefully tatty clothing, the slender, unexpectedly bare midriff; quite obviously it's Tina, Kaeti's crazy, fragile friend. "Get her," I said urgently. "Get her, she's vital...." No need to point out who. The Goddess of the Garden had already been noted; a decade or more of working together obviates the need to spell things out, verbal shorthand serves as well. I turned on my heel, made tracks in the opposite direction. There are times, and this was one of them, when the presence of gawpers is strictly surplus to requirements.

A friend in Amesbury considers the image thoughtfully. "She's like the young Liz Taylor," he says. "Same face shape." It's right; and him not even an artist! There are other things though. Her glance seems to be sliding sidelong; impossible to be sure whether or not she's aware of the distant camera, even with the print in front of us.

If she is, she doesn't care. She's only accepting her dues; Goddesses are there for worshipping. The slim leads of a Walkman show at her neck. So she isn't sleeping rough after all, despite the careful costuming; those things come expensive. Don chuckles. "One thing you can be sure of anyway. She's not listening to a Classical tape."
"On the contrary. She's a piano student from Royal College, taking a day off. She's playing Rachmaninov."
"Is that a fact?"
"It may well be. Prove I'm wrong." London is full of surprises; if she was listening to punk, that would be the real letdown.

I must be crazy, hanging my wall with pictures of girls I don't know. But they're not pictures of girls, as far as I'm concerned; they're simply Images. Anyway, I don't know who the old lacemaker was either. It must be my artistic side coming out. Once, conveying my lady mother to her place of torment (she was a nursing auxiliary; the torment, undoubtedly, was suffered by the patients) she snatched a letter from the glove compartment of the car. It was addressed to a woman in Manchester; I had forgotten to post it. "Who is this?"
"I don't know."
A familiar expression crossed her face; the mixture of contempt and irritability with which she greeted anything that lay outside her immediate understanding. Which amounted to quite a lot.
"Nobody writes letters to people they don't know."
"She wrote an enquiry about a thing I did. She put an s.a.e. in, so I answered it. I don't know who she is."
The matriarch remains suspicious. "I still say you don't write to total strangers."
"Well my dear, if total strangers are the only ones who show an interest in what I do, I don't have much option, do I?"
Clang.... In fact I spent years writing to people I didn't know. They call it being an author. But I don't bother to make the point. She wouldn't understand that either.

I get busy with a mitre block, take the results along to a man recommended to me for the cutting of glass. He has a small shop in a Salisbury side street. He peers at the stack of frames and sniffs. "Make 'em yourself then?"

I'm well aware of the shortcomings of my handiwork. But I'm also aware of what that lot would have set me back at commercial rates. There are times when one has to cut one's suit according to the cloth.
"I don't have a guillotine. A blind man'd be pleased to see 'em though."
He's OK. I was told he was. He says I'm welcome to buy framing material from him if I feel like doing any more. And the glass

will be ready in the afternoon. I leave feeling moderately acquitted. At least the exhibition can be mounted. It's to proceed through the flat from hall to loo, with a branch into the bedroom. I fell for an ormolu frame in the two-story flea market the city boasts. The lady who sold it to me said she had the devil's own job stripping the coat of aluminium paint with which some previous owner had thoughtfully improved it. After she'd gone to so much trouble it seemed only right to give it a good home; and it's exactly right for a postcard of Munch's "Pubertiet" that I'd had stored away. I saw the original once; I wouldn't want it reproduced any larger. Not and have to live with it at least. A bare girl sits quaking on a bed. She casts an obtrusive shadow. Within the scumble of paint lurks the dreary face of a lecher; he has been called into being by the Fact of her existence. It's a final grim comment on the condition of woman.

It's also a first-rate figure study. The ultimate Expressionist was no slouch in the Life class of course; before he deserted reality in his attempt, as he put it, to paint the unpaintable.

When I first moved to Waitrose-on-Thames I got heavily involved in the local amateur theatricals. I rapidly found out the drawbacks. All that was really wanted was somebody who could stick wires into plugs; the town's celebrities could tread the boards then unencumbered by such minor irritations. But stage lighting led to set design and a whole lot besides. Also, with each show I did it seemed the opposition built up; it was the origin of my remark about success being the unforgiveable crime. It culminated with the local Operatic Society, a body of stunning ineptness, dragging a set out of the scene store and burning it, to prevent my using it for anybody else. I was moderately annoyed; but the show I was currently working on involved devising half a dozen stagings, one more made very little odds. Later though I decided there must be better ways of not earning a living. I would spend my free time writing; that way I wouldn't have anybody else poking their noses in, initially at least. While production problems likewise wouldn't be my concern. I found it didn't exactly work like that. An old form master at Kettering Grammar, a bitter and acerbic man, was fond of remarking that the drawback to having brains was that we would find ourselves continually being forced to use them. At the time I found a degree of comfort in the notion. If true, it meant that at least I would never be short of work. What he omitted to point out was that we wouldn't necessarily get anything for our efforts; apart from brickbats of course.

Being honest, I suppose the initial fault was mine every time for getting involved in the first place. But the stage was there to be lit, the same as stories were there to be written. And books seemed to demand to be produced. A certain siren lure was involved. The ears of most folk seemed to be stopped effectively enough; what I really needed was a helpful crewman to tie me to the mast. This time though I could surely sit back, regard my collection of trophies and the distant prospect of the Cathedral and leave the hassle to others. There could be no harm in that.

Ten years before my removal to Amesbury had seen the millennium of the foundation of Elfrida's Abbey. To celebrate the event, the Amesbury Society had agreed to the production of a book on the village and its history; I had been loaned a copy shortly after my arrival, and had been much impressed. So often in that sort of project, good intentions outrun skill; in this case the co-authors had done their job conscientiously and well. I read the text avidly. So many new facts to learn; who would have thought for instance that the strange little building on the corner of the High Street, now the premises of an estate agent, was once the village lockup? Or that the site of the local cinema, still functioning though soon to be closed, was first occupied by a Bioscope show? Over all was the shadow of Catherine Queensbury, the Countess Kitty of popular memory, who provided all the estate tenants with warm chairs, and who once invited the great Dean Swift to visit for the express purpose of discovering a fault in his allegedly perfect nature. One day I would have to write a story about her; Kaeti would surely have understood her, very well.

A decade after publishing the History, a reprint had been decided on. It coincided with my arrival on the scene. Not surprisingly, the negatives had not been retained by the original printer. So a resetting was called for, something not without advantages. The somewhat dubious typeface could be replaced by a decent font; while the opportunity had been taken to enlarge and update the text. The thing would be even more valuable now.

What was also needed was a cover design for what would this time be a paperback. An update seemed called for there as well; something more positive than the pleasant but unassuming layout that had been used the first time, certainly. "What you really want is something you can use as a point of sale display; you could run a couple of hundred extra when you print the job, it wouldn't cost that much more. It would pay for itself; you'll be selling in libraries as well as bookshops, there ought to be a lot of local interest."

Don supplies population figures for Amesbury, Andover, and Salisbury, Mass. With the American interest in roots, the promotion possibility seems heaven-sent. "Get the local Chambers of Commerce involved. You'd be in for a reprint before you knew where you were."

I stop abruptly. I once observed to my colleague that the day I turned my toes up he would come knocking on the box lid, asking if he could have an eight-inch double by Tuesday. He agreed mildly that it was more than likely. That's the thing about advertising though; after a while it gets to be automatic. You're involved then before you know where you are.

The authors agree to pass on the suggestion. But they won't do more. After all, they've just spent months revising the damned book; their wives will be pleased enough to have the dining room tables clear of papers. By their tone, they don't have a great deal of confidence. To be truthful, neither do I. But weeping for lost causes could easily become a full time job. First things first; what's needed is a cover visual.

I go through a copy of the first edition. One of the many illustrations seems a natural; a view along the High Street toward the old London Road, not built up at the time and fringed with woods. I'd date the photograph at somewhere about nineteen ten or twelve, mainly on the evidence of the splendid motor drawn up outside Richard Dickeson & Sons' establishment. The owner sits proudly aloft. I wonder who he was. Local landowner perhaps; he evidently wasn't short of a bob or two. Come to that, who were Richard Dickeson & Sons? Hauliers I should think; two of their wagons are standing in the street, at the moment minus their horses. They haven't been brought round from the stables yet; or maybe it's the lunch hour, they're taking a well-earned break. There are hills on most of the roads out of town, they'll have been doing some heavy pulling. Another cart has halted farther along the street. It's small with distance, but its driver still poses beside it optimistically. Like all old photographs, the picture invites contemplation. Because all the people you can see are ghosts.

Peter Goodhugh arrives at the flat. He's a careful, incisive man; a founder member of the Society, and one of the book's two authors. The cover design met with general approval; more than that, they're dead keen to have it. But there's just one problem.

"Don't tell me, let me guess. You don't have a neg for the photograph I used."

He spreads out a variety of prints, a little apologetically. He did his best, re-negging the faded postcard; some of the results are interesting, but they won't do for the wraparound layout I proposed. At that size the image dies on its feet. So there's only one answer, and we both know what it is. He shakes his head. "I didn't like to ask...."

"It's all right. I painted myself into a corner; I shall just have to draw my way back out of it." The artwork will have to be produced by hand; I estimate the job time at about forty hours. I'd been prepared for the eventuality; the only problems that tend to throw you are ones that haven't been foreseen. And then you're more annoyed at yourself, for not having allowed for them. Leastways, that's how it seems to work with me.

I go round to see the printer who is doing the job. He runs a smart, modern little works a few yards from Salisbury city center. I ask him if he can give me a duotone. He nods. "No problem. It'll be interesting actually; we've never been asked for one before. What were you hoping to do with it?"

"I want a sepia effect. It'll be a lot better with a duotone, if we can get the second color right. A single plate would just look washed out."

He nods. "I know what you mean. It happened with the photographs in the book. We could have done a lot better if we'd processed them individually. It wasn't on though, it would have cost a couple of pounds extra for every neg. Maybe two fifty. So we just had to push the button and let 'em go through."

I'm well satisfied. This is a man who knows his job, and takes a pride in it. But there's some neat registration work on his compliment slip that already told me that. Somehow a shadow of the old Guilds still seems to hang about much of the printing trade; it's been there ever since Gutenberg of Mainz cast letters onto little blocks of metal, and invented reusable type. It saved the Keroseenies when their first printer went down the tube, though I doubt it registered much with them. That sort-of thing doesn't, not to folk who've become legends in their own lunchtimes. I suffered some moments of doubt myself, though my colleague was quietly confident. "They'll be looked after. The trade as a whole isn't let to suffer. You'll see." He was right, as ever.

The duotone process isn't seen so much now; which is a pity, because it has many applications. I used it for the wrapper of my ghost collection, with blue as the second color to enhance the eerie effect. Two plates are prepared from a single image; the screen is rotated between exposures, so the halftone dots don't coincide. I've never actually used it for a drawing; but I see no reason why it shouldn't work. Neither does the helpful man who is to oversee the job. A Pantone chart is produced; I settle for an orange-yellow ink. What I have to visualize is the effect when combined with the black plate.

"It won't matter all that much. We'll proof it anyway; if it isn't right we can always change it, and proof again." My helper is keen on the job himself. This is basically a trade house; the finished book will be a useful specimen to have, it's a bit outside their usual range of work.

The second color is right. Dead right. In fact the proof takes me aback a little; it has exactly the glowing quality I wanted, the unique glow of an old sepia print. The world that had been frozen in that long-ago moment comes to curious life. Long puddles lie in the gutters; but the windows of most of the cottages stand open. There has been rain the night before, heavy rain; now the sky is overcast, the morning humid. The drawing I prepared was really just a start; the magic of process photography has taken over.

So I was really a phoney myself. I wasn't in touch with Higher Things at all, more a sort of—well, a tradesman. Talking to printers and copywriters and the like, using the same language.... That's OK though. My Dad was a tradesman; and Gutenberg, Joe Haydn, and a fair few more. I reckon I could have been in worse company.

IX.

Liz pops the passbook into the nearest of the machines, enters the details of the transaction. As usual, I watch the deft movements of her hands. They are slender; as she is slender, and tall. Her blonde hair hangs forward in a cloud. She suffers the same problem a lot of English women have; it's lovely hair, but fine. Lacks bulk. So last week she got fed up and had it permed. She didn't announce the fact, not in as many words; but then, she hardly needed to. The result spoke for itself; her crowning glory has developed a life of its own, as she works she has to push it back continually. A clip would help; or a wooden Alice band, the sort of thing Lemady often wore.

Lemady was well aware her hair was a major asset; and that she was fortunate. Hair that is full and thick is often coarse in texture; that's a cross the Mediterranean women in particular have to bear. It's all a question of checks and balances; and of course the art that conceals art. But that's something the PH, the Primitive Heroine, always knew.

That last was a little taradiddle of my own; leastways Robert Holdstock, who entered the PH stakes enthusiastically, told me I was the one who devised the term, though I was never wholly sure. To an extent it was deceptive; certainly anybody who assumed the creatures we dreamed up, or more accurately perhaps defined in print, were lacking in sophistication, radically misunderstood the breed, perhaps the very nature of woman herself. Liz would be the same in any age; like Tam, and Kaeti, and Lucia Queen. In one of her last stories, leastways the last in which she took a central part before handing over to her loquacious daughter Norma, Kaeti was sold in a Londinium slave market. Naturally, the process didn't appeal; but loss of freedom was only part of the problem. It was the way it was done that galled; being knocked down like a suspect bunch of grapes from a street trader's stall was her real complaint. There should have been veils and stuff, a bit of presentation. After all, if you're going to meet a fate worse than death, at least do it in style. Dressed in skins, she would have been the same. Not perhaps the highest of *couture*; but what was this year's hemline? Was it to be on the knee, or that critical fraction above? Or was it to be the maxi look again? These thing matter a great deal; they are as vital, and eternal, as woman herself.

I'm well aware of course that I'm straying into the realms of fantasy. Certainly I'm not seriously suggesting that Crô-Magnon females had their preferred fashion designers. To apply such a radically modern frame of thinking would be to commit the very crime against logic of which I complained at length a few pages back. What I do sense though is a more subtle continuity. Surrounded by the machinations of Hollywood, Guinevere loses none of her power; rather, it is enhanced. It was a principle Treece assumed more or less throughout his writing, though the savage times he largely dealt with ensured its continual submergence. What's important is that it resurfaced, time and again. The endless wryness of the archetypal dollybird character argues a certain mental sturdiness; that and a sometimes desperate resilience that in itself characterizes the humor of the endlessly-suffering Jewish race. "I've got some good news and some bad," announces the secretary in the hoary but still amusing joke. "Which do you want first?" Her boss opts for the good news. It consists of the information that he's not sterile. It's the sort of line Kaeti might well come out with; or Lemady.

The question of hair has always been a vexed issue; from the days of Samson onwards, and doubtless for a fair time before. No wonder they built a whole musical round it once. Some of the numbers were good, though the show itself I could well have left alone. The non-stop din induced a species of combat fatigue; on the trip home I all but dozed off, despite the presence of a vividly attractive companion. While as for the staging I'd heard lauded to the skies; a group of not very prepossessing young people writhing about under a sheet, to emerge finally minus their knickers, hardly amounted to a *coup de théâtre* as far as I was concerned. But maybe by that time I was getting jaundiced. Though as my colleague once remarked, it's the age of the amateur. Originally the word meant a lover of a craft; but the point would seem to have been lost.

When I was a lad in the Midlands, girls cut their hair on marriage. It was considered the proper thing to do. Leastways it was a convention that was seldom if ever flouted. It seems fairly obvious that what they were basically doing was signalling their non-available status by reduction of their sexual charms, though it's unlikely the thought was formalized as such. Later, growing the hair beyond the traditional collar length became a symbol of liberation for young men in the so-called swinging sixties; but old habits die hard, old thought patterns even harder. Working in a Maidenhead ad agency a decade on, I was reminded sharply that the prohibition was still alive and well. A middle-aged woman in the so-called media section—her job was to paste an endless selection of small ads into a large scrapbook, so at a need it could be proved to a suspicious client that the insertions had taken place—called my attention to a pretty girl walking in the street below the office windows. She wore a cheerful, vivid mini; she was wheeling an infant in a push chair, and her hair hung nearly to her waist. "Look at that," said the old trout. "Look at that, Mr. Roberts. That's disgusting...." For a moment I thought she meant the dress; but it was the hair. "She ought to have it *cut*," she hissed. "Looks terrible, going about like that...."

"But why? It isn't dirty or anything. I thought how nice it was."

"Oh, it isn't *dirty*. But it ought to be *cut*...." I pressed her for some further explanation; but she became evasive and confused, finally annoyed. I had ventured onto forbidden ground.

Something similar once happened with my old friend Wattie. Made aware of the ban, which apparently was new to her, Lemady had vowed never to cut her hair again; for all I know, she never did. "Yon bliddy lassie," the accentless Scot, was already out of favor; but the information was greeted by an explosion spectacular even by Wattie's standards. "It's no' a subject for a man's conversation...." Later, a mutual acquaintance explained the reason for the eruption. Wattie's daughter, a pretty girl by all accounts and very much the apple of his eye, had recently become engaged to a young man of whom he sharply disapproved; and the new *fiancé* was a hair stylist. Once again, I escaped with my life; but I always seemed to be sailing close to the wind with Wattie.

I once wrote a small monograph on the *Natural History of the P.H.* It wasn't exactly done with serious intent; but when it was suggested it be published as what the fans insist on calling a chapbook, the chance seemed too good to miss. The great Mucha was about to come into public domain; his famous poster "Cycles Perfecta" would furnish a splendid cover design, while my colleague's flair for typography could once more be brought into play. The result was highly satisfying; but one piece of verbal shorthand could well have been expanded. Hair primped, permed, or generally messed about with, I opined, may indicate many things; but its owner was not, and could never be, a genuine P.H. For "perm" read the dreadful hairstyles of the forties, the original Permanent Waves. Occasionally something of the sort is still, shudderingly, to be seen. "Merciless as steel swarf" was Kaeti's reaction to one such silvered hairdo; in the story, and the real event on which the episode was based, the description matched the mentality of the owner. She claimed to have been an Air Raid Warden during World War Two. "'Ave you ever scraped bits o' people orf the path with a shovel? There ain't a German fit ter live. No, nor a Jap." "There's nobody quite as merciless as a law-abiding citizen with a legal excuse for violence," observes the pagan general Stilicho in my Roman epic, *The Boat of Fate*. "It's a trait of the civilized world I've never particularly admired...."

A keen sense of the femaleness of certain women argues of course detestation of its opposite. The costume styles of the Thirties and Forties were equally dire: the military cut of blouses, the harsh, exaggerated padding of jackets. Many women's clothes are padded, even relatively light garments, I'm well aware of that; but no less a luminary than Christian Dior once came to my aid. "I have devalued the shoulder," he proclaimed, introducing his soft, gently elegant New Look. It was seen as an antidote to the austerities of World War Two; it was an antidote to a good deal else beside.

For the modern equivalent of the "Permanent" I have nothing but respect. Molly Zero changed her hairstyle, and more importantly its color, to go with the raggle-taggle gypsies. It was an event of critical importance to her; I accordingly made extensive notes of the process that would be involved, consulting an ex-hairdresser friend for the purpose. She was more than helpful; but she was also intrigued. "What do you want to *know* for?" she demanded. "Why do you want to know all this?" On the face of things, the answer was simple. I was working on the principle outlined by Rafael Sabatini: writers should know at least ten times more about their subject than they propose to use. That way there's a chance of the result carrying conviction at least. But there was a little more than that. My character, who had appeared so arbitrarily it seemed as an answer to an irritating distraction, had begun to lead a life of her own. She was about to change her psyche, no less. For her, it was to be a vital event; so it was no less vital to me. The story had "taken fire."

Any heroine, whether overtly Primitive or otherwise, is the product of artifice, startling as the notion might seem to the young or jejeune. It's a part of her essential nature. In the extraordinary Russian film *Solaris*, the planetary entity creates a simulacrum of the psychiatrist's dead wife. She was picked out of his brain, made up from his own memories; is she therefore "real?" If not, then was the Edwardian chorine a figment of the imagination? It would have taken a brave man, I feel, to say so to her face. Would the girl in front of me somehow become more vital, more immediate, if you dowsed her with a bucket of water? But Liz, still trying to control the wild mane created for her by Art, would seem to have little time for the farther reaches of philosophy.

She presses a button. The machine begins to emit a series of high pitched machine-gun rattlings. I would be a bit wary of touching it. As somebody remarked once, he was afraid to fiddle with the controls of a large American car in case he dropped an H-bomb. Liz doesn't seem concerned though; she folds her arms, and waits for the sounds of mechanical mayhem to cease.

So exactly what would an unbiased observer see? A graceful blonde girl certainly, with a piquant, vivid face. I see that much of course; but there seems a great deal more. A quality perhaps, some essence of femaleness; to me, she is the ideal. The Perfect Girl, glimpsed perhaps for the very first time; the ultimate magic, sprung at last from the ultimately magic place. The lines of an old song go through my mind; not thought about for years, but charged now with a new and heightened meaning.

Where'er you walk, cool gales shall fan the glade.
Trees where you sit, shall crowd into a shade...

I consider. The man who wrote those glittering words was in love. So that's what it feels like; I've never been too sure.

I did do one brief story about a computer, strictly as the result of a commission. No doubt the artist I devised as a protagonist would have been expected to smash the thing, like some latter-day Luddite. My antipathy would have been presumed, as it was once presumed I objected on principle to fanzines and the people who produced them. In the event, it was the machine that had the measure of the man. If my mind was really closed it would be so much easier for the whizzkids to categorize me. Not that it will hold them back; they'll pigeonhole me anyway. Ramming pegs into their holes, regardless of whether or not they fit, is their chief preoccupation; maybe it's their defense against reality. I've seen it claimed the increasing formality of French landscape art, culminating in the straightjacketed perfection of places like Versailles, was a last attempt to impose a spurious order in face of the mounting horror of the Revolution to come. Psychologically, it seems a touch on the obvious side; but the idea is engaging nonetheless.

The title I finally devised for my little piece was "Measured Perspective." It referred to an exercise we indulged in as part of our art school course. We drew a plan of the building proposed, dropped verticals to a picture plane, established vanishing points to either side, and so on. After a couple of hours' work we were rewarded by a perspective rendering of a plain, shoebox-shaped little church; if a slightly different angle was required, the whole process had to be gone through again. A while ago on television I watched a simulated flight over an American city. Perspectives of buildings rushed toward me, fell away breathlessly. To produce such a thing by the old methods would take not just years, but lifetimes. The old dream had come true; final release from the drudgery of calculation. I'd like to know more about the new techniques, as would my colleague. It takes real computer men to write programs like that though; elimination of birdcage graphics was just a stage along the way. I still feel there's a chance I could talk to them, and get sense back in return; because they would speak plain English.

Instead, I write a piece of cover blurb. The whizzkid who is to publish it feeds it into a bulky device that dominates the sitting room table. He presses a couple of buttons, hands it across with a flourish. The copy has been turned into a narrow, justified column.

151

"Oh. What's that for?"

He is patient. "To show you what it will look like."

"I see. So what will it look like? What will your typeface be? What's the point size? What measured will you use? Leaded, or set solid?"

I could go on of course. Roman or Italic, bold face, medium or light; but there would seem to be little point. He has already done his bit; he's turned the copy into a column. Effortlessly as well, by the simple pressing of buttons. That should be enough for any reasonable person. Much better to play with his pieces of paper, woffle on about Computer Literacy. The rest's for those printer johnnies to sort out. It's boring; worse, he'd run the risk of getting his toes wet.

The machine set into the counter gives a final determined *zip* and disgorges the passbook. Liz checks it briefly and tucks the cash into it. She smiles, and pushes it back under the bandit screen. I resented the barriers when they first began to be installed, in common I suppose with a lot of folk. It was instructive though scarcely encouraging to watch the change in attitude of many of the staff. Customers ceased to be real people, with needs to be met; instead the clerks developed the habit of staring past and through them. It was a sort of reversed goldfish-bowl effect. We were the pieces of decorative fauna, theirs the real, enclosed world. Now though I'm glad of the defense. I could wish there was another: a great steel thing that would shoot up with a clang if danger threatened, to keep her safe. There's a vulnerability to her situation that gives rise to something almost like panic. There was a girl in Bremen once who featured her a little; but she was caught by hoodlums. They dragged her across Europe for a day and night, the focus of a swarm of pressmen; then they shot her through the head and heart.

I'd heard about it of course, caught the newscast that announced the desolate affair was over. I'd felt sorry in an abstract way, but that was all. It's not given to ordinary mortals to take on the griefs of the world; our own are usually more than enough for us. In any case, next day was going to be a busy one for me. I was bound for Waitrose-on-Thames, to the marriage of the girl who once refused to enter beauty contests. On the coach I got into conversation with an engaging young man who sported a shock of vivid auburn hair. He asked me if I had met many redheaded Italians. His grandfather had fought with the Eighth Army, from Africa to Berlin. On the way he fell in love with an Italian girl; after the war he returned and married her, and the family had been bilingual ever since. Now, my informant feels it might be a useful skill to have.

The latter-day Vivaldi debarks at Heathrow. He leaves his morning paper with me. Glancing at it idly, I wonder what such a lovely girl has been doing to get herself onto the front page. Then I see

152

the gun at her neck, and realization comes far too late. Had it not been for a pair of murderous junkies I would never have known of her existence, never seen her name in print. I shall certainly never see it again.

The day that followed was a curious one for me. Despite myself, images clashed continually. My friends' daughter, the girl I had known for so long, radiant in unexpected white; Concorde booming above the little church, *en route* for the Woodley beacon; a cold room in another country, where a blonde girl lay under a sheet. What would they use to hide the bullet holes, graft on the semblance of peace? Something more than greasepaint would seem to be called for; maybe pan makeup's the thing though, for morgues. I know they put lint knickers on the corpses, "for modesty's sake," as I once heard it grindingly expressed; and the thin blood withdrawn by the so-called embalming process is poured down loos.

Before quitting the town I absentmindedly withdraw some cash. The girl at the counter is red-haired, and vividly attractive; I haven't seen her for the best part of a year. She asks if they're looking after me down south.

"Yes, fine thanks. No problems." I look round. "They haven't got your glamour lineup though."

She grins. "Thank you, kind sir...." A few days later, Liz arrives. I feel I'm well served out.

The estimate of job time on the new book cover wasn't far out; though if anything I erred on the low side. Forty-five hours would have been safer for the whole thing. Forty-five hours of anybody's time except an illustrator, anyway. But that's the trouble about creative work, so-called; quite literally, it's invaluable. At one extreme, anything that's priced at all leads to righteous indignation. I once produced a pastel painting of their pub for my innkeeping friends, framed it for them as a Chrissie Pressie. It was for services rendered, though they weren't to know just how much psychological help they'd been over the years. It was hung proudly in the saloon bar; a few days later I was asked the question I had been expecting. Several people in the village had expressed an interest in having their love nests immortalized in similar fashion; purely for curiosity, what would I charge for a job like that?

As it happened, I had already worked it out. So had Mine Host. It hadn't been all that time-consuming; in any case there are ways and means of cutting corners. Some legitimate, others less so. Add the cost of framing material, a bit of glass; at half the rate a car mechanic would charge it came to fifty quid. I passed the information over, and as also expected heard no more. What, pay that for a *sketch*? A fiver would have been closer to their expectations; or five bob. On the other hand, there's the story of the manufacturers of art materials who wanted to improve their image. So they went to one of the best known Agencies in the country. Would it be advisable to update the typeface stamped on all their pencils? Turned out it was not; they were charged 20K for the consultation, and presumably went their way rejoicing. The story of the King's new clothes had received another update. The real value? Like I said to my erstwhile employer, it's somewhere in between.

Peter Goodhugh was quite shrewd enough to have estimated the job time on the new artwork, probably with some accuracy. Though nothing was said directly. A few copies handed over in the car park after the launch ceremony—how often such small niceties acquire a hole-and-corner, vaguely illicit air—later an unexpected but much apppreciated *pourboire*, and that was the end of the affair.

For my part, I hadn't been looking for a return. Just for once the job was its own reward, plus. Amesbury was another place that had been entwined in my awareness for as long as I cared to remember; but the notion that one day I would lay my hand to such a project was one that had not occurred. How could it? Such a thing lay in the lap of the Gods; or a Goddess. In the story of Kaeti and the Sky Person, her great benefactress unloads a chunk of granite that had lain by her throne since the Blitz of World War Two, to the detriment of the baddie's Rolls-Royce; it was one of the little asides that particularly horrified the Adviser whose thankless job it was to set me straight. You just can't do that sort of thing; leastways, unless you've made a few bob for the company first. Then, all sorts of lapses become excusable; at the worst, they can always be blamed on creativity. My piece of debris had been sailing through the air for nearly the same length of time; luckily for me, the landing was a lot more gentle.

"In my craft, or sullen art..." Dylan Thomas was talking about the writing process of course; but the description would apply equally well to graphics. Or I suppose a number of solitary occupations; fretwork, the making of cuckoo clocks. In my case there wasn't as a rule much sullenness involved in producing artwork. A certain unwillingness to get started perhaps, when I knew I was in for a long and not particularly rewarding stint; but there were compensations. Something pleasant on the radio, the knowledge that this week at least one was going to be able to eat and pay one's rent; playing the part of a small town advertising artist, Kaeti admitted to similar feelings once her neat behind was settled onto a draughtsman's stool.

I get stuck into the Amesbury job. The old High Street grows slowly; Dickeson and Sons, the New Inn, massive Tudor chimney stacks of the George. Wheel ruts on the unmade road, the squat post, rope-scarred, that had guarded the corner properties from the wheels of passing carts. All is there to be rendered; along with the puddled gutters, the many little opened windows. Some casemented, some, as the French say, *à guillotine*. By degrees my mind peoples the street with

154

the folk of a bygone time; a process aided no doubt by the sprightly little annual carnivals the town holds, with their recurrent Victorian and Edwardian themes.

A mechanical organ plays from the back of a flatbed truck; everywhere are boaters and high collars, the swirl of silk and muslin.

In time, as the pencil point moves steadily, delineating textures of stone and brick, one image comes to dominate. She is elegant, and tall; she carries a cheeky parasol, and her hat is decked with flowers. Gingham would suit her, I decide; gingham checked and countryfied. Mentally I allow her a slim choker ribbon; and at the back not a bustle but a little bow, remnant of that once-bizarre fashion. So delicate, so graceful; it will enhance her slenderness. Somewhere, brooding, not so far off, are the stones of the Great Henge; but she belongs there too. She the heir of all the ages, in the foremost rank of Time. She swirls the parasol, glances up with her humorous, almond-tilted eyes; and by degrees the thing is finished. I indicate the bleed trims, tick in the title and ISBN placings, mark the job for reduction and take it to the printer. So that's that; what's next on the list?

I stow the pass book in my wallet, turn to leave; but my Special, it seems, has not finished yet. "'Scuse, Mr. Roberts; could I ask you a question?"

Ask away, my love; it seems to be the week for them. Why, only the other evening I was quizzed at length as to the color of my blood. Was it really blue inside me, and only red when it came out? I paused, gravely. Hard to make out the inquisitor; the sun was setting, all I could see was a neat, tousle-headed silhouette. But she sat at a focus of magic, where the great ley that runs past Stonehenge and Clearbury Rings crosses the Salisbury water meadows; so an answer must be made, and that carefully.

Obviously she had had an argument with her biology master. I leafed mentally through the school notes I once took, on the vascular system and all the rest. She listened carefully, as I had known she would, and thanked me; but as I moved away along the Town Path a yell of triumph rose. "There you are," she shouted at her companions, "I told you I was right...." I was arrested again. Inconsequential the incident might well have been, pointless to some perhaps; but in that instant a new personality had been born. I would call her Norma.

Liz smiles, and pops her question. "Are you an artist?" she says.

I open my mouth, and close it. All the hours, days, months, spent at the drawing board; if added together, I suppose they would total years. Does that qualify me? All the missed chances, opportunities ruined by others or by circumstance; the tiny triumphs, so rapidly forgotten by me as well as by everybody else; do they make me what she said? Trekking to Avebury with Tam, with Lemady, wearing a track to Purbeck in summer heat, in snow; awareness gained by slow degrees, Mucha, *La Belle Époque*, Paul Nash floundering in Flanders mud; could such things be written in? Realization of perfection; could that be added to the scales? Could I perhaps claim a hint of aesthetic awareness?

She's still smiling; but there's nothing of mockery there. Nor will there be; because the Perfect Girl doesn't mock. It's not permitted her; she has responsibilities, as Lucia Queen was bound by duty to her subjects. Dubious philosophy, even more dubious logic; but I'd like to think it would have afforded the Gotama at least the ghost of a smile. Perhaps Queen Pasenadi too.

Well, it's a busy branch; I can't stand here gawping all day. I find a voice from somewhere. A sort of a voice at least.

"I do do artwork, yes...."

She nods, well satisfied. She whips a copy of the Amesbury book from beneath the counter. "This came in the other day. I saw the signature. The others wondered if it was our Mr. Roberts. I said next time you came in, I'd find out." She turns the book. "I think the drawing's absolutely beautiful. I can just imagine myself walking along the street, standing on the corner...."

There's something here that needs thinking through. I make my escape, head for my favorite bar. My head's buzzing slightly; but one thing is already clear. It's a new world, and I'm a new person; my body molecules, the fluids, salts, and all the rest, have changed three times over since that last jagged meeting so many years ago. But Lemady is back; in a sense, perhaps she never went away.

INDEX

167